Monologues from Shakespeare's First Folio for Younger Men: *The Histories*

The Applause Shakespeare Monologue Series

Other Shakespeare Titles From Applause

Once More unto the Speech Dear Friends
Volume One: The Comedies
Compiled and Edited with Commentary by Neil Freeman

Once More unto the Speech Dear Friends
Volume Two: The Histories
Compiled and Edited with Commentary by Neil Freeman

Once More unto the Speech Dear Friends
Volume Three: The Tragedies
Compiled and Edited with Commentary by Neil Freeman

The Applause First Folio in Modern Type
Prepared and Annotated by Neil Freeman

The Folio Texts
Prepared and Annotated by Neil Freeman, Each of the 36 plays of the
Applause First Folio in Modern Type individually bound

The Applause Shakespeare Library
Plays of Shakespeare Edited for Performance

Soliloquy: The Shakespeare Monologues

Monologues from Shakespeare's First Folio for Younger Men: *The Histories*

Compilation and Commentary by
Neil Freeman

Edited by
Paul Sugarman

APPLAUSE
THEATRE & CINEMA BOOKS

Guilford, Connecticut

APPLAUSE
THEATRE & CINEMA BOOKS

An imprint of Globe Pequot, the trade division of
The Rowman & Littlefield Publishing Group, Inc.
4501 Forbes Blvd., Ste. 200
Lanham, MD 20706
www.rowman.com

Distributed by NATIONAL BOOK NETWORK

Library of Congress Cataloging-in-Publication Data available

Library of Congress Control Number: 2021944369

ISBN 978-1-4930-5690-3 (paperback)
ISBN 978-1-4930-5691-0 (ebook)

♾™ The paper used in this publication meets the minimum requirements of
American National Standard for Information Sciences—Permanence of Paper for
Printed Library Materials, ANSI/NISO Z39.48-199

Dedication

Although Neil Freeman passed to that "undiscovered country" in 2015, his work continues to lead students and actors to a deeper understanding of Shakespeare's plays. With the exception of Shakespeare's words (and my humble foreword), the entirety of the material within these pages is Neil's. May these editions serve as a lasting legacy to a life of dedicated scholarship, and a great passion for Shakespeare.

Contents

FOREWORD

Paul Sugarman

Monologues from Shakespeare's First Folio presents the work of Neil Freeman, longtime champion of Shakespeare's First Folio, whose groundbreaking explorations into how first printings offered insights to the text in rehearsals, stage and in the classroom. This work continued with *Once More Unto the Speech Dear Friends: Monologues from Shakespeare's First Folio with Modern Text Versions for Comparison* where Neil collected over 900 monologues divided between the Comedy, History and Tragedy Published by Applause in three masterful volumes which present the original First Folio text side by side with the modern, edited version of the text. These volumes provide a massive amount of material and information. However both the literary scope, and the literal size of these volumes can be intimidating and overwhelming. This series' intent is to make the work more accessible by taking material from the encyclopediac original volumes and presenting it in an accessible workbook format.

To better focus the work for actors and students the texts are contrasted side by side with introductory notes before and commentary after to aid the exploration of the text. By comparing modern and First Folio printings, Neil points the way to gain new insights into Shakespeare's text. Editors over the centuries have "corrected" and updated the texts to make them "accessible," or "grammatically correct." In doing so they have lost vital clues and information that Shakespeare placed there for his actors. With the texts side by side, you can see where and why editors have made changes and what may have been lost in translation.

In addition to being divided into Histories, Comedies, and Tragedies, the original series further breaks down speeches by the character's designated gender, also indicating speeches appropriate for any gender. Drawing from this example, this series breaks down each original volume into four workbooks: speeches for Women of all ages, Younger Men, Older Men and Any Gender. Gender is naturally fluid for Shakespeare's characters since during his time, ALL of the characters were portrayed by males. Contemporary productions of Shakespeare commonly switch character genders (Prospero has become Prospera), in addition to presenting single gender, reverse gender and gender non-specific productions. There are certainly characters and speeches where the gender is immaterial, hence the inclusion of a volume of speeches for Any Gender. This was something that Neil had indicated in the original volumes; we are merely following his example.

The monologues in the book are arranged by play in approximate order of composition, so you get his earliest plays first and can observe how his rhetorical art developed over time. The speeches are then arranged by their order in the play.

Once More Unto the Speech Dear Friends was a culmination of Neil's dedicated efforts to make the First Folio more accessible and available to readers and to illuminate for actors the many clues within the Folio text, as originally published. The material in this book is drawn from that work and retains Neil's British spelling of words (i.e. capitalisation) and his extensive commentary on each speech. Neil went on to continue this work as a master teacher of Shakespeare with another series of Shakespeare editions, his 'rhythm texts' and the ebook that he published on Apple Books, *The Shakespeare Variations*.

Neil published on his own First Folio editions of the plays in modern type which were the basis the Folio Texts series published by Applause of all 36 plays in the First Folio. These individual editions all have extensive notes on the changes that modern editions had made. This material was then combined to create a complete reproduction of the First Folio in modern type, *The Applause First Folio of Shakespeare in Modern Type*. These editions make the First Folio more accessible than ever before. The examples in this book demonstrate how the clues from the First Folio will give insights to understanding and performing these speeches and why it is a worthwhile endeavour to discover the riches in the First Folio.

PREFACE AND BRIEF BACKGROUND TO THE FIRST FOLIO

WHY ANOTHER SERIES OF SOLILOQUY BOOKS?

There has been an enormous change in theatre organisation recent in the last twenty years. While the major large-scale companies have continued to flourish, many small theatre companies have come into being, leading to

- much doubling
- cross gender casting, with many one time male roles now being played legitimately by/as women in updated time-period productions
- young actors being asked to play leading roles at far earlier points in their careers

All this has meant actors should be able to demonstrate enormous flexibility rather than one limited range/style. In turn, this has meant

- a change in audition expectations
- actors are often expected to show more range than ever before
- often several shorter audition speeches are asked for instead of one or two longer ones
- sometimes the initial auditions are conducted in a shorter amount of time

Thus, to stay at the top of the game, the actor needs more knowledge of what makes the play tick, especially since

- early plays demand a different style from the later ones
- the four genres (comedy, history, tragedy, and the peculiar romances) all have different acting/textual requirements
- parts originally written for the older, more experienced actors again require a different approach from those written for the younger

ones, as the young roles, especially the female ones, were played by young actors extraordinarily skilled in the arts of rhetoric

There's now much more knowledge of how the original quarto and folio texts can add to the rehearsal exploration/acting and directing process as well as to the final performance.

Each speech is made up of four parts

- a background to the speech, placing it in the context of the play, and offering line length and an approximate timing to help you choose what might be right for any auditioning occasion
- a modern text version of the speech, with the sentence structure clearly delineated side by side with
- a folio version of the speech, where modern texts changes to the capitalization, spelling and sentence structure can be plainly seen
- a commentary explaining the differences between the two texts, and in what way the original setting can offer you more information to explore

Thus if they wish, **beginners** can explore just the background and the modern text version of the speech.

An actor experienced in exploring the Folio can make use of the background and the Folio version of the speech

And those wanting to know as many details as possible and how they could help define the deft stepping stones of the arc of the speech can use all four elements on the page.

The First Folio

(FOR LIST OF CURRENT REPRODUCTIONS SEE BIBLIOGRAPHY

The end of 1623 saw the publication of the justifiably famed First Folio (F1). The single volume, published in a run of approximately 1,000 copies at the princely sum of one pound (a tremendous risk, considering that a single play would sell at no more than six pence, one fortieth of F1's price, and that the annual salary of a schoolmaster was only ten pounds), contained thirty-six plays.

The manuscripts from which each F1 play would be printed came from a variety of sources. Some had already been printed. Some came from the playhouse complete with production details. Some had no theatrical input at all, but were handsomely copied out and easy to read. Some were supposedly very messy, complete with first draft scribbles and crossings out. Yet, as Charlton Hinman, the revered dean of First Folio studies describes F1 in the Introduction to the Norton Facsimile:

> It is of inestimable value for what it is, for what it contains. For here are preserved the masterworks of the man universally recognized as our greatest writer; and preserved, as Ben Jonson realized at the time of the original publication, not for an age but for all time.

WHAT DOES F1 REPRESENT?

- texts prepared for actors who rehearsed three days for a new play and one day for one already in the repertoire
- written in a style (rhetoric incorporating debate) so different from ours (grammatical) that many modern alterations based on grammar (or poetry) have done remarkable harm to the rhetorical/debate quality of the original text and thus to interpretations of characters at key moments of stress.
- written for an acting company the core of which steadily grew older, and whose skills and interests changed markedly over twenty years as well as for an audience whose make-up and interests likewise changed as the company grew more experienced

The whole is based upon supposedly the best documents available at the time, collected by men closest to Shakespeare throughout his career, and brought to a single printing house whose errors are now widely understood - far more than those of some of the printing houses that produced the original quartos.

TEXTUAL SOURCES FOR THE AUDITION SPEECHES

Individual modern editions consulted in the preparation of the Modern Text version of the speeches are listed in the Bibliography under the separate headings 'The Complete Works in Compendium Format' and ' The Complete Works in Separate Individual Volumes.' Most of the modern versions of the speeches are a compilation of several of these texts. However, all modern act, scene and/or line numbers refer the reader to The Riverside Shakespeare, in my opinion still the best of the complete works despite the excellent compendiums that have been published since.

The First Folio versions of the speeches are taken from a variety of already published sources, including not only all the texts listed in the 'Photostatted Reproductions in Compendium Format' section of the Bibliography, but also earlier, individually printed volumes, such as the twentieth century editions published under the collective title *The Facsimiles of Plays from The First Folio of Shakespeare* by Faber & Gwyer, and the nineteenth century editions published on behalf of The New Shakespeare Society.

INTRODUCTION

So, congratulations , you've got an audition, and for a Shakespeare play no less.

You've done all your homework, including, hopefully , reading the whole play to see the full range and development of the character.

You've got an idea of the character, the situation in which you/it finds itself (the given circumstance s); what your/its needs are (objectives/ intentions); and what you intend to do about them (action /tactics).

You've looked up all the unusual words in a good dictionary or glossary; you've turned to a well edited modern edition to find out what some of the more obscure references mean.

And those of you who understand metre and rhythm have worked on the poetic values of the speech, and you are word perfect . . .

. . . and yet it's still not working properly and/or you feel there's more to be gleaned from the text , but you're not sure what that something is or how to go about getting at it; in other words, all is not quite right, yet.

THE KEY QUESTION

What text have you been working with - a good modern text or an 'original' text, that is a copy of one of the first printings of the play?

If it's a modern text, no matter how well edited (and there are some splendid single copy editions available, see the Bibliography for further details), despite all the learned information offered, it's not surprising you feel somewhat at a loss, for there is a huge difference between the original printings (the First Folio, and the individual quartos, see

Appendix 1 for further details) and any text prepared after 1700 right up to the most modern of editions. All the post 1700 texts have been tidied-up for the modern reader to ingest silently, revamped according to the rules of correct grammar, syntax and poetry. However the 'originals' were prepared for actors speaking aloud playing characters often in a great deal of emotional and/or intellectual stress, and were set down on paper according to the very flexible rules of rhetoric and a seemingly very cavalier attitude towards the rules of grammar, and syntax, and spelling, and capitalisation, and even poetry.

Unfortunately, because of the grammatical and syntactical standardisation in place by the early 1700's, many of the quirks and oddities of the origin also have been dismissed as 'accidental' - usually as compositor error either in deciphering the original manuscript, falling prey to their own particular idosyncracies, or not having calculated correctly the amount of space needed to set the text. Modern texts dismiss the possibility that these very quirks and oddities may be by Shakespeare, hearing his characters in as much difficulty as poor Peter Quince is in *A Midsummer Night's Dream* (when he, as the Prologue, terrified and struck down by stage fright, makes a huge grammatical hash in introducing his play 'Pyramus and Thisbe' before the aristocracy, whose acceptance or otherwise, can make or break him)

> If we offend, it is with our good will.
> That you should think, we come not to offend,
> But with good will.
>   To show our simple skill,
> That is the true beginning of our end .
> Consider then, we come but in despite.
> We do not come, as minding to content you ,
> Our true intent is.
>   All for your delight
> We are not here.
>   That you should here repent you,

> The Actors are at hand; and by their show,
> You shall know all, that you are like to know.

(A Midsummer Night's Dream)

In many other cases in the complete works what was originally printed is equally 'peculiar,' but, unlike Peter Quince , these peculiarities are usually regularised by most modern texts.

However, this series of volumes is based on the belief - as the following will show - that most of these 'peculiarities' resulted from Shakespeare setting down for his actors the stresses, trials, and tribulations the characters are experiencing as they think and speak, and thus are theatrical gold-dust for the actor, director, scholar, teacher, and general reader alike.

THE FIRST ESSENTIAL DIFFERENCE BETWEEN THE TWO TEXTS

THINKING

A **modern** text can show

- the story line
- your character's conflict with the world at large
- your character's conflict with certain individuals within that world

but because of the very way an 'original' text was set, it can show you all this plus one key extra, the very thing that makes big speeches what they are

- the conflict within the character

WHY?

Any good playwright writes about characters in stressful situations who are often in a state of conflict not only with the world around them and the people in that world, but also within themselves. And you probably know from personal experience that when these conflicts occur people do not necessarily utter the most perfect of grammatical/poetic/ syntactic statements, phrases, or sentences. Joy and delight, pain and sorrow often come sweeping through in the way things are said, in the incoherence of the phrases, the running together of normally disassociated ideas, and even in the sounds of the words themselves.

The tremendous advantage of the period in which Shakespeare was setting his plays down on paper and how they first appeared in print was that when characters were rational and in control of self and situation, their phrasing and sentences (and poetic structure) would appear to be quite normal even to a modern eye - but when things were going wrong, so sentences and phrasing (and poetic structure) would become highly erratic. But the Quince type eccentricities are rarely allowed to stand. Sadly, in tidying, most modern texts usually make the text far too clean, thus setting rationality when none originally existed.

THE SECOND ESSENTIAL DIFFERENCE BETWEEN THE TWO TEXTS
SPEAKING, ARGUING, DEBATING

Having discovered what and how you/your character is thinking is only the first stage of the work - you/it then have to speak aloud, in a society that absolutely loved to speak - and not only speak ideas (content) but to speak entertainingly so as to keep listeners enthralled (and this was especially so when you have little content to offer and have to mask it somehow - think of today 's television adverts and political spin doctors as a parallel and you get the picture). Indeed one of the Elizabethan 'how to win an argument' books was very precise about this - George Puttenham, *The Art of English Poesie* (1589).

A: ELIZABETHAN SCHOOLING

All educated classes could debate/argue at the drop of a hat, for both boys (in 'petty-schools') and girls (by books and tutors) were trained in what was known overall as the art of rhetoric, which itself was split into three parts

- first, how to distinguish the real from false appearances/outward show (think of the three caskets in *The Merchant of Venice* where the language on the gold and silver caskets enticingly, and deceptively, seems to offer hopes of great personal rewards that are dashed when the language is carefully explored, whereas once the apparent threat on the lead casket is carefully analysed the reward therein is the greatest that could be hoped for)

- second, how to frame your argument on one of 'three great grounds'; honour/morality; justice/legality; and, when all else fails, expedience/practicality.

- third, how to order and phrase your argument so winsomely that your audience will vote for you no matter how good the opposition - and there were well over two hundred rules and variations by which winning could be achieved, all of which had to be assimilated before a child's education was considered over and done with.

B: THINKING ON YOUR FEET: I.E. THE QUICK, DEFT , RAPID MODIFICATION OF EACH TINY THOUGHT

The Elizabethan/therefore your character/therefore you were also trained to explore and modify your thoughts as you spoke - never would you see a sentence in its entirety and have it perfectly worked out in your mind before you spoke (unless it was a deliberately written, formal public declaration, as with the Officer of the Court in The Winter' s Tale, reading the charges against Hermione). Thus after uttering your very first phrase, you might expand it, or modify it, deny it, change it, and so on throughout the whole sentence and speech.

From the poet Samuel Coleridge Taylor there is a wonderful description of how Shakespeare puts thoughts together like "a serpent twisting and untwisting in its own strength," that is, with one thought springing out of the one previous. Treat each new phrase as a fresh unravelling of the serpent's coil. What is discovered (and therefore said) is only revealed as the old coil/phrase disappears revealing a new coil in its place. The new coil is the new thought. The old coil moves/disappears because the previous phrase is finished with as soon as it is spoken.

C: MODERN APPLICATION

It is very rarely we speak dispassionately in our 'real' lives, after all thoughts give rise to feelings, feelings give rise to thoughts, and we usually speak both together - unless

1/ we're trying very hard for some reason to control ourselves and not give ourselves away

2/ or the volcano of emotions within us is so strong that we cannot control ourselves, and feelings swamp thoughts

3/ and sometimes whether deliberately or unconsciously we colour words according to our feelings; the humanity behind the words so revealed is instantly understandable.

D: HOW THE ORIGINAL TEXTS NATURALLY ENHANCE/ UNDERSCORE THIS CONTROL OR RELEASE

The amazing thing about the way all Elizabethan/early Jacobean texts were first set down (the term used to describe the printed words on the page being 'orthography'), is that it was flexible, it allowed for such variations to be automatically set down without fear of grammatical repercussion.

So if Shakespeare heard Juliet's nurse working hard to try to convince Juliet that the Prince's nephew Juliet is being forced to (bigamously) marry, instead of setting the everyday normal

'O he's a lovely gentleman'

which the modern texts HAVE to set, the first printings were permitted to set

'O hee's a Lovely Gentleman'

suggesting that something might be going on inside the Nurse that causes her to release such excessive extra energy.

E: BE CAREFUL

This needs to be stressed very carefully: the orthography doesn't dictate to you/force you to accept exactly what it means. The orthography simply suggests you might want to explore this moment further or more deeply.

In other words, simply because of the flexibility with which the Elizabethans/Shakespeare could set down on paper what they heard in their minds or wanted their listeners to hear, in addition to all the modern acting necessities of character - situation, objective, intention, action, and tactics the original Shakespeare texts offer pointers to where feelings (either emotional or intellectual, or when combined together as passion, both) are also evident.

SUMMARY

BASIC APPROACH TO THE SPEECHES SHOWN BELOW

(after reading the 'background')

1/ first use the modern version shown in the first column: by doing so you can discover

- the basic plot line of what's happening to the character, and
- the first set of conflicts/obstacles impinging on the character as a result of the situation or actions of other characters
- the supposed grammatical and poetical correctnesses of the speech

2/ then you can explore

- any acting techniques you'd apply to any modern soliloquy, including establishing for the character
- the given circumstances of the scene
- their outward state of being (who they are sociologically, etc.)
- their intentions and objectives
- the resultant action and tactics they decide to pursue

3/ when this is complete, turn to the First Folio version of the text, shown on the facing page: this will help you discover and explore

- the precise thinking and debating process so essential to an understanding of any Shakespeare text
- the moments when the text is NOT grammatically or poetically as correct as the modern texts would have you believe, which will in turn help you recognise
- the moments of conflict and struggle stemming from within the character itself
- the sense of fun and enjoyment the Shakespeare language nearly always offers you no matter how dire the situation

4/ should you wish to further explore even more the differences between the two texts, the commentary that follows discusses how the First Folio has been changed, and what those alterations might mean for the human arc of the speech

NOTES ON HOW THESE
SPEECHES ARE SET UP

For each of the speeches the first page will include the Background on the speech and other information including number of lines, approximate timing and who is addressed. Then will follow a spread which shows the modern text version on the left and the First Folio version on the right, followed by a page of Commentary.

PROBABLE TIMING: (shown on the Background page before the speeches begin, set below the number of lines) 0.45 = a forty-five second speech

SYMBOLS & ABBREVIATIONS IN THE COMMENTARY AND TEXT

F: the First Folio

mt.: modern texts

F # followed by a number: the number of the sentence under discussion in the First Folio version of the speech, thus F #7 would refer to the seventh sentence

mt. # followed by a numb er: the number of the sentence under discussion in the modern text version of the speech, thus mt. #5 would refer to the fifth sentence

 # /#, (e.g. 3/7): the first number refers to the number of capital letters in the passage under discussion; the second refers to the number of long spellings therein

within a quotation from the speech: / indicates where one verse line ends and a fresh one starts

[ ] : set around words in both texts when Fl sets one word , mt another

{ } : some minor alteration has been made, in a speech built up, where, a word or phrase will be changed, added, or removed

{†} : this symbol shows where a sizeable part of the text is omitted

TERMS FOUND IN THE COMMENTARY
OVERALL

1/ **orthography**: the capitalization, spellings, punctuation of the First Folio
SIGNS OF IMPORTANT DISCOVERIES/ARGUMENTS WITHIN A FIRST FOLIO SPEECH

2/ **major punctuation**: colons and semicolons: since the Shakespeare texts are based so much on the art of debate and argument, the importance of F1 's major punctuation must not be underestimated, for both the semi-colon (;) and colon (:) mark a moment of importance for the character, either for itself, as a moment of discovery or revelation, or as a key point in a discussion, argument or debate that it wishes to impress upon other characters onstage

as a rule of thumb:

a/ the more frequent colon (:) suggests that whatever the power of the point discovered or argued, the character is not side-tracked and can continue with the argument - as such, the colon can be regarded as a **logical** connection

b/ the far less frequent semicolon (;) suggests that because of the power inherent in the point discovered or argued, the character is side-tracked and momentarily loses the argument and falls back into itself or can only continue the argument with great difficulty - as such, the semicolon should be regarded as an **emotional** connection

3/ **surround phrases**: phrase(s) surrounded by major punctuation, or a combination of major punctuation and the end or beginning of a sentence: thus these phrases seem to be of especial importance for both character and speech, well worth exploring as key to the argument made and /or emotions released

DIALOGUE NOT FOUND IN THE FIRST FOLIO
∞ set where modern texts add dialogue from a quarto text which has not been included in Fl

A LOOSE RULE OF THUMB TO THE THINKING PROCESS OF A FIRST FOLIO CHARACTER

1/ mental discipline/**intellect:** a section where capitals dominate suggests that the intellectual reason ing behind what is being spoken or discovered is of more concern than the personal response beneath it

2/ feelings/**emotions:** a section where long spellings dominate suggests that the personal response to what is being spoken or discovered is of more concern than the intellectual reasoning behind it

3/ **passion:** a section where both long spellings and capitals are present in almost equal proportions suggests that both mind and emotion/feelings are inseparable, and thus the character is speaking passionately

SIGNS OF LESS THAN GRAMMATICAL THINKING WITHIN A FIRST FOLIO SPEECH

1/ **onrush:** sometimes thoughts are coming so fast that several topics are joined together as one long sentence suggesting that the F character's mind is working very quickly, or that his/her emotional state is causing some concern: most mod ern texts split such a sentence into several grammatically correct parts (the opening speech of *As You Like It* is a fine example, where F's long 18 line opening sentence is split into six): while the modern texts' resetting may be syntactically correct, the F moment is nowhere near as calm as the revisions suggest

2/ **fast-link:** sometimes F shows thoughts moving so quickly for a character that the connecting punctuation between disparate topics is merely a comma, suggesting that there is virtually no pause in springing from one idea to the next: unfortunately most modern texts rarely allow this to stand, instead replacing the obviously disturbed comma with a grammatical period, once more creating calm that it seems the original texts never intended to show

FIRST FOLIO SIGNS OF WHEN VERBAL GAME PLAYING HAS TO STOP

1/ **non-embellished:** a section with neither capitals nor long spellings suggests that what is being discovered or spoken is so important to the character that there is no time to guss it up with vocal or mental excesses: an unusual moment of self-control

2/ **short sentence:** coming out of a society where debate was second nature, man y of Shakespeare's characters speak in long sentences in which ideas are stated, explored, redefined and summarized all before moving onto the next idea in the argument, discovery or debate: the longer sentence is the sign of a rhetorically trained mind used to public speaking (oratory), but at times an idea or discovery is so startling or inevitable that length is either unnecessary or impossible to maintain : hence the occasional very important short sentence suggests that there is no time for the niceties of oratorical adornment with which to sugar the pill - verbal games are at an end and now the basic core of the issue must be faced

3/ **monosyllabic:** with English being composed of two strands, the polysyllabic (stemming from French, Italian, Latin and Greek), and the monosyllabic (from the Anglo-Saxon), each strand has two distinct functions: the polysyllabic words are often used when there is time for fanciful elaboration and rich description (which could be described as 'excessive rhetoric') while the monosyllabic occur when, literally, there is no other way of putting a basic question or comment - Juliet's "Do you love me? I know thou wilt say aye" is a classic example of both monosyllables and non-embellishment: with monosyllables, only the naked truth is being spoken, nothing is hidden

Monologues from Shakespeare's First Folio for Younger Men: *The Histories*

The Second Part of Henry the Sixt
Suffolke

Madame, my selfe have lym'd a Bush for her,
1.3.88–100

Background: since Suffolke must remove Gloster from power if the shared ambitions he and Margaret have for their eventual governance of England are to come to fruition, a two pronged attack will be extremely useful. Here, in response to Margaret's outburst he explains his plans to destroy Gloster's wife, the over ambitious Elianor, in part by joining forces with the untrustworthy Cardinall (Beauford), also an enemy to Gloster.

Style: as part of a two-handed scene

Where: unspecified, a public space in or near the palace

To Whom: Margaret

# of Lines: 13

Probable Timing: 0.45 minutes

Take Note: Again, F's sentence structure and orthography suggest the concerns and cautions through which Suffolke operates. Most modern texts' reworking of F's sentence structure and inability to show F's orthographic subtleties create a far more one-dimensional speech than originally set.

Suffolke

1   Madam , myself have lim'd a bush for her,
     And plac'd a choir of such enticing birds
     That she will light to listen to [their] lays ,
     And never mount to trouble you again .

2   So let her rest ; and, madam , list to me,
     For I am bold to counsel you in this .

3   Although we fancy not the Cardinal ,
     Yet must we join with him and with the lords,
     Till we have brought Duke Humphrey in disgrace .

4   As for the Duke of York , this late complaint
     Will make but little for his benefit .

5   So one by one we'll weed them all at last,
     And you your self shall steer the happy helm .

Suffolke

1   Madame, my selfe have lym'd a Bush for her,
    And plac't a Quier of such enticing Birds,
    That she will light to listen to [the] Layes,
    And never mount to trouble you againe .

2   So let her rest : and Madame list to me,
    For I am bold to counsaile you in this ;
    Although we fancie not the Cardinall,
    Yet must we joyne with him and with the Lords,
    Till we have brought Duke Humphrey in disgrace .

3   As for the Duke of Yorke, this late Complaint
    Will make but little for his benefit :
    So one by one wee'le weed them all at last,
    And you your selfe shall steere the happy Helme .

- the surround phrases opening F #2 emphasise that the anti-Elianor plot, cut and dried as it is, is not Suffolke's prime concern: the awkward joining forces with another of Margaret's antagonists, the Cardinall, is—emphasised even more by the link of the only (emotional) semicolon (end of line 2 F #2)

- the onrush as their need for the Cardinall is first mentioned (F #2) and then the out and out dismissal of another enemy, the Duke of York (F # 3), suggests some urgency (reassuring Margaret perhaps? and/or a measure of his own confidence?) : this is very much diminished by the modern texts' splitting each sentence into two

- at first glance the speech seems quite passionate (13/15 in thirteen lines), yet there are two contrasting clusters—7 of the 13 capitals defusing both enemies (the three lines ending F #2 and the opening of #3), and 4 of the 15 long spellings come as Suffolke predicts their eventual success in the last two lines of the speech

The Second Part of Henry the Sixt
King

Stand forth Dame Elianor Cobham,
2.3.1–13 & 22–27

Background: Suffolke's plot (see previous speech) has worked to perfection, and Elianor has been arrested by Yorke (leader of the opposing enemy family) with seemingly incriminating statements as to the future life and death of King Henry, as well as about Suffolke and the leader of the Lancastrian faction, Somerset. Here, Henry passes judgment on his Uncle's wife, and those caught with her.

Style: public sentencing of five people in front of a highly interested group of observers

Where: a place of state, perhaps a hall of justice

To Whom: Elianor; the witch Marjery Jordan; the conjuror Bullingbroke; and the two priests, Hume and Southwell, caught with her (i.e. the 'foure' referred to in line 6) in front of at least Margaret, Gloster, Suffolke, and Yorke. (Modern texts often add Buckingham, Salisbury, and attendants.)

# of Lines: 20

Probable Timing: 1.00 minutes

Take Note: In altering F's line structure as well as sentence count, modern texts remove all the difficulties the F1 Henry has in passing such devastating judgements, not just on the necromancers, but more especially on his Aunt (Elianor) and Uncle (Gloster).

King

1 Stand forth Dame [Eleanor] Cobham, [Gloucester's]
                                      wife :
  In sight of God and us, your guilt is great ;
  Receive the sentence of the law for [sins]
  Such as by God's book are adjudg'd to death .

2 You four , from hence to prison back again ;
  From thence, unto the place of execution.

3 The witch in Smithfield shall be burnt to ashes,
  And you three shall be strangled on the gallows .

4 You, madam , for you are more nobly born ,
  Despoiled of your honor in your life,
  Shall, after three days' open penance done,
  Live in your country here in banishment,
  With Sir John [Stanley], in the [Isle] of Man .

5 Stay, [Humphrey], Duke of [Gloucester] !

6   Ere thou go ,
  Give up thy staff .

7   Henry will to himself
  Protector be, and God shall be my hope,
  My stay, my guide, and lanthorn to my feet ;
  And go in peace, [Humphrey], no less belov'd
  [Than] when thou wert Protector to thy king.

King

1   Stand forth Dame [Elianor] Cobham,
     [Glosters] Wife :
     In sight of God, and us, your guilt is great,
     Receive the Sentence of the Law for [sinne],
     Such as by Gods Booke are adjudg'd to death .

2   You foure from hence to Prison, back againe ;
     From thence, unto the place of Execution :
     The Witch in Smithfield shall be burnt to ashes,
     And you three shall be strangled on the Gallowes .

3   You Madame, for you are more Nobly borne,
     Despoyled of your Honor in your Life,
     Shall, after three dayes open Penance done,
     Live in your Countrey here, in Banishment,
     With Sir John [Stanly], in the [Ile] of Man .

---

4   Stay [Humfrey], Duke of Gloster,
     Ere thou goe, give up thy Staffe,
     Henry will to himselfe Protector be,
     And God shall be my hope, my stay, my guide,
     And Lanthorne to my feete :
     And goe in peace, [Humfrey], no lesse belov'd,
     [Then] when thou wert Protector to thy King .

- despite the preponderance of capitals (36) to long spellings (17) Henry is still undergoing a great deal of personal strain

- F's opening pair of split lines suggests that Henry has difficulty in calling his aunt forward: most modern texts set the two lines as one

- while the speech opens with apparent control (at least as regards the images used—10/1 in F #1), at the moment of sentencing the lesser lights to death (the last line of F #1 and the opening of F #2), three long spellings intrude

- interestingly, while the sentencing of his aunt seems to cause little public personal release (12/6 in the five lines of F #3) , the irregular line structure stripping his uncle of his cherished role as Protector (F #4, see below) seems a heavier emotional task for Henry (10/7 in seven lines)

- for in closing, F #4, the F text is set as five irregular lines (7/7/10/10/6 syllables) which suggests that Henry has great difficulty formulating the necessary words as he strips his Uncle of political office: the modern texts reset the passage as 4 regular lines, each of ten syllables, thus making the task much easier, at least oratorically

The Second Part of Henry the Sixt

King

What, doth my Lord of Suffolke comfort me ?
3.2.39–55

Background: Gloster's death, or rather murder, has deeply upset Henry and all those loyal to him. Margaret and Suffolke try to comfort him in the open Court, and finally Henry's contempt and anger towards the man publicly acknowledged to be his wife's lover breaks forth. Henry has just recovered after fainting at the news of his uncle Gloster's death, and the following is triggered by Suffolke's 'Comfort my soveraigne, gracious Henry comfort'.

Style: five-handed scene in front of a larger group via concentration on one person

Where: the English court in London

To Whom: Suffolke, in front of Queene Margaret, Beauford, Somerset, and Attendants

# of Lines: 17

Probable Timing: 0.55 minutes

Take Note: Henry's disturbed response to the news of the death of his Uncle and (until recently) Protector, Gloster, is evident in the modern text. What F adds is where his control breaks, at first understandably, and then where his self-composure disappears completely.

King

1   What, doth my Lord of Suffolk comfort me ?

2   Came he right now to sing a raven's note,
Whose dismal tune bereft my vital pow'rs ;
And thinks he that the chirping of a wren,
By crying comfort from a hollow breast,
Can chase away the first-conceived sound ?

3   Hide not thy poison with such sug'red words.

4   Lay not thy hands on me ; forbear , I say !
Their touch affrights me as a serpent's sting .

5   Thou baleful messenger, out of my sight !

6   Upon thy eye-balls murderous tyranny
Sits in grim majesty , to fright the world .

7   Look not upon me, for thine eyes are wounding :
Yet do not go away .

8   Come, basilisk ,
And kill the innocent gazer with thy sight ;
For in the shade of death, I shall find joy ;
In life, but double death, now [Gloucester's] dead .

King

1   What, doth my Lord of Suffolke comfort me ?

2   Came he right now to sing a Ravens Note,
Whose dismall tune bereft my Vitall powres :
And thinkes he, that the chirping of a Wren,
By crying comfort from a hollow breast,
Can chase away the first-conceived sound ?

3   Hide not thy poyson with such sugred words,
Lay not thy hands on me : forbeare I say,
Their touch affrights me as a Serpents sting .

4   Thou balefull Messenger, out of my sight :
Upon thy eye-balls, murderous Tyrannie
Sits in grim Majestie, to fright the World .

5   Looke not upon me, for thine eyes are wounding ;
Yet doe not goe away : come Basiliske,
And kill the innocent gazer with thy sight :
For in the shade of death, I shall finde joy ;
In life, but double death, now [Gloster's] dead .

- the opening two sentences match, but, though the passion to be expected in such a public attack on his wife's murderer-lover is present (6/4 in the first four and a half F lines), the speech then takes an interesting turn

- Henry's calling out of Suffolke's tactics (the last two lines of F #2) is totally non-embellished, an unusual moment of self-control for a normally more emotional character

- indeed, personal feelings supplant any intellectual discipline in the first two lines of F #3 (0/2), and then mental order is restored until the end of F #4 (5/1 in just four lines) as he orders Suffolke out of his sight

- so far, the quick switches in spoken release and mental/emotional control are to be expected, especially given the circumstances of the scene

- however, F sentence #5 suggests that having now had a long hard look at Suffolke, what he discovers destroys his self composure, for the five lines contain no fewer than four heavy pieces of punctuation (including two emotional semi-colons) which quite terrifyingly turn all five lines of the sentence into surround phrases: it seems, especially with the weirdly contrasting thoughts and the final wish for death, F's orthography suggests that Henry is undergoing some form of brainstorm or even mental breakdown

The Second Part of Henry the Sixt

King

Goe Salisbury, and tell them all from me,
between 3.2.279–300

Background: Henry's immediate response to Salisbury's speech, in which he banishes Suffolke and publicly rebukes Margaret, whom he knows is Suffolke's lover.

Style: initially a public address to one man, for the benefit of a larger group, and then to his wife

Where: the English court in London

To Whom: first Salisbury and then Margaret, in front of Suffolke, Warwicke, Beauford, Somerset, and Attendants

# of Lines: 20

Probable Timing: 1.00 minutes

Take Note: Once more the opening of the two texts match, but, as with Henry's previous speech, F's orthography clearly indicates where the underlying stress gets the better of him.

King

1   Go , Salisbury, and tell them all from me,
     I thank them for their tender loving care ;
     And had I not been cited so by them,
     Yet did I purpose as they do entreat ;
     For sure, my thoughts do hourly prophesy ,
     Mischance unto my state by Suffolk's means .

2   And therefore by His majesty I swear ,
     Whose far -unworthy deputy I am,
     He shall not breathe infection in this air
     But three days longer, on the pain of death .

---

3   Ungentle queen , to {plead for 'gentle'} Suffolk !

4   No more, I say !

5   If thou dost plead for him,
     Thou wilt but add increase unto my wrath .

6   Had I but said , I would have kept my word ;
     But when I swear , it is irrevocable .

7   If after three days space thou here be'st found,
     On any ground that I am ruler of,
     The world shall not be ransom for thy life .

8   Come, Warwick , come, good Warwick , go with me ,
     I have great matters to impart to thee .

King

1   Goe Salisbury, and tell them all from me,
     I thanke them for their tender loving care ;
     And had I not beene cited so by them,
     Yet did I purpose as they doe entreat :
     For sure, my thoughts doe hourely prophecie,
     Mischance unto my State by Suffolkes meanes .

2   And therefore by his Majestie I sweare,
     Whose farre-unworthie Deputie I am,
     He shall not breathe infection in this ayre,
     But three dayes longer, on the paine of death .

---

3   Ungentle Queene, to {pleade for 'gentle'} Suffolke .

4   No more I say : if thou do'st pleade for him,
     Thou wilt but adde encrease unto my Wrath .

5   Had I but sayd, I would have kept my Word ;
     But when I sweare, it is irrevocable :
     If after three dayes space thou here bee'st found,
     On any ground that I am Ruler of,
     The World shall not be Ransome for thy Life .

6   Come Warwicke, come good Warwicke, goe with mee,
     I have great matters to impart to thee .

- F's setting of Henry's quieting of his wife as just one sentence (#4) shows much more meltdown than the modern texts which split the sentence in two (mt. #4-5) and add an exclamation mark (end mt. #4), suggesting a much more controlled and powerful rejection than F: the breaking up of the same F onrush (mt. #6-7 replacing of F's #5) suggests similar control not offered in the original text

- here, there are twice as many emotional long spellings as capital letters (14/28)

- the two (emotional) semicolons show that no matter how determined Henry's determination may be to deal with Suffolke, there is still a highly personal cost

- his determination is also highlighted by the three surround phrases,

  " . No more I say : "

  and

  ". Had I but sayd, I would have kept my Word ; /But when I sweare, it is irrevocable : "

- 11 of the 14 capital letters are found in just three clusters, and while two of them focus on Henry's decision to banish Suffolke plus his need to plan further, and the decision's fall-out on his marriage

  "Ungentle Queene, to {pleade for 'gentle'} Suffolke"

  and

  "If…thou here bee'st found,/On any ground that I am Ruler of,/The World shall not be Ransome for thy Life ./Come Warwicke, come good Warwicke, goe with mee,"

  the latter part of the third

  "And therefore by his Majestie I sweare,/Whose farre-unworthie Deputie I am,"

  tends to support Margaret's earlier complaints of his over-religious zeal

The Second Part of Henry the Sixt

Jack Cade

Up Fish-streete, downe Saint Magnes corner,
4.8.1–5 & 20–32

Background: the rebel Jack Cade, presenting himself as Mortimer, the rightful heir to the throne (who, though with a legitimate claim, died in prison) having swept through the South-East of England is now wreaking murderous havoc in London itself. The royalists Buckingham and Clifford meet his forces and attempt to appeal to their loyalty by invoking the glorious memories of the time of the much beloved Henry V. The following is how Cade mishandles the situation.

Style: public address, to two opposing monarchists and an unspecified number of his own men

Where: in the streets of London

To Whom: Buckingham, Clifford, and Cade's own rebel forces

# of Lines: 17

Probable Timing: 1.00 minutes

Take Note: F's orthography and minor sentence variations add more depth to an already colourful character.

Cade

1   Up Fish-street ! down Saint [Magnus'] corner !
     kill and knock down ! throw them into Thames !

> **Sound a parley**

2   What noise is this I hear ?

3   Dare any be so bold to sound
     retreat or parley when I command them kill ?

4   What, Buckingham and Clifford, are ye so brave ?

5   And you, base peasants, do ye believe him ?

6   Will you needs
     be hang'd with your pardons about your necks ?

7   Hath
     my sword therefore broke through London gates, that
     you should leave me at the White Hart in [Southwark]?

8   I thought ye would never have given [over] these armstill
     you had recovered your ancient freedom .

9   But you are
     all recreants and dastards, and delight to live in slavery
     to the nobility .

10   Let them break your backs with bur-
     thens, take your houses over your heads, ravish your
     wives and daughters before your faces .

11   For me, I will
     make shift for one ; and so God's curse light upon you
     all !

Cade

1   Up Fish-streete, downe Saint [Magnes] corner,
kill and knocke downe, throw them into Thames{:}

      Sound a parley

What noise is this I heare ?

2   Dare any be so bold to sound Retreat or Parley
When I command them kill ?

---

3   What Buckingham and Clifford are ye so brave ?

4   And you base Pezants, do ye beleeve him, will you needs
be hang'd with your Pardons about your neckes ?

5   Hath
my sword therefore broke through London gates, that
you should leave me at the White-heart in [Southwarke] .

6   I thought ye would never have given [out] these Armes til
you had recovered your ancient Freedome .

7   But you are
all Recreants and Dastards, and delight to live in slaverie
to the Nobility .

8   Let them breake your backes with bur-
thens, take your houses over your heads, ravish your
Wives and Daughters before your faces .

9   For me, I will
make shift for one, and so Gods Cursse light uppon you
all .

- while the opening two and a half lines of the speech are highly passionate (4/5) they are not plagued by the four exclamation marks that most modern texts have added, thus suggesting that he starts with speed and enjoyment, not just a generalised unfocused yell

- though at the (shaded) end of sentence #1 and all of #2, F switches to irregular verse (6/13/6 syllables - perhaps suggesting that Cade suddenly assumes a public swagger and bravado in facing down a perceived challenge, so as to substantiate his pretend role as the noble John Mortimer, claimant to the throne), most modern texts, arguing white space, maintain the opening prose, with at least one text omitting the Ff phrase 'I heare', claiming it to be compositorial invention

- and surprisingly, given the circumstances of his men abandoning him, the remainder of the speech contains almost twice as many capitals (16) as long-spellings (9)

- with the arrival of the Lordly enemy leaders and Cade's challenge first to them (F #2-3) and then to his men (F #4-5) , he uses a highly intellectual approach (9/3 in six lines), perhaps suggesting his need to argue carefully to get his points across, or, more likely, over-confidence

- but then, in disbelief that his men have changed sides so easily (F #6), passion breaks through again (2/2 in one and a half lines)

- then, as he begins to curse his men out (F #7), intellect momentarily returns (3/0 in one and a half lines)

- and as he finishes the curse, extending it to their families, and vows to seek for his own safety (F's #8-9, ending the speech), so passion breaks through again (4/4)

The Second Part of Henry the Sixt

Jack Cade

Was ever Feather so lightly blowne too & fro,
4.8.55 - 65

Background: Buckingham and Clifford finally win over Cade's forces, arguing that only their surrender to the King (without any punishment to follow) can protect them from supposed invasion by the French (a highly spurious invention if ever there was one). Thus Cade is forced to flee.

Style: solo, even though surrounded by many from two opposing groups

Where: in the streets of London

To Whom: direct audience address, in the midst of his own men who have just surrendered to the royalist forces

# of Lines: 10

Probable Timing: 0.35 minutes

Take Note: As with Cade's prior speech, F's orthography and minor sentence variations add more depth to an already colourful character.

Cade

1 Was ever feather so lightly blown too & fro
   as this multitude ?

2   The name of Henry the Fift hales them
   to an hundred mischiefs, and makes them leave me de-
   solate .

3   I see them lay their heads together to surprise
   me .

4   My sword make way for me, for here is no staying .

5 In despite of the devils and hell, have through the very*
   middest of you !

6   And heavens and honor be witness that
   no want of resolution in me, but only my followers
   base and ignominious treasons, makes me betake me to
   my heels.

Cade

1   Was ever Feather so lightly blowne too & fro,
as this multitude ?

2   The name of Henry the fift, hales them
to an hundred mischiefes, and makes them leave mee de-
solate .

3   I see them lay their heades together to surprize
me .

4   My sword make way for me, for heere is no staying :
in despight of the divels and hell, have through the verie
middest of you, and heavens and honor be witnesse, that
no want of resolution in mee, but onely my Followers
base and ignominious treasons, makes me betake mee to
my heeles .

- the extra breaths from the two extra commas in F #1-2 might suggest Cade's astonishment at his men's desertion

- with 2 of the 3 capitals occurring in the first two sentences, the rest of the speech is almost completely emotional (1/10 in six lines of F #3-4)

- as he begins his escape, the one surround phrase ' . My sword make way for me, for heere is no staying : ' sets up a much longer sentence ending the speech than set in modern texts, which split it into three: the F text suggests far more determination and perhaps energy/difficulty in getting through the mob than the modern texts show

*The Third Part of
Henry the Sixt*

Messenger

The Noble Duke of Yorke {is} slaine,
2.1.46–67

Background: the only speech for the character; as such it is self-explanatory.

Style: direct address to three men, in front of a larger group

Where: in the open in Herefordshire

To Whom: Yorke's three sons, Edward, George, and Richard, in front of their forces

# of Lines: 20

Probable Timing: 1.00 minutes

Take Note: F's orthography and sentence structure present not only the message but also the humanity of the Messenger, for it seems s/he cannot stay completely unattached—as the speech develops, so his/her feelings start to flood the delivery of the facts.

Messenger

1   {†} {T}he noble Duke of York {is} slain,
    Your princely father and my loving lord !

2   Environed he was with many foes,
    And stood against them, as the hope of Troy
    Against the Greeks that would have ent'red Troy .

3   But Hercules himself must yield to odds;
    And many strokes, though with a little axe,
    Hews down and fells the hardest-timber'd oak.

4   By many hands your father was subdu'd,
    But only slaught'red by the ireful arm
    Of unrelenting Clifford and the queen :
    Who crown'd the gracious Duke in high despite,
    Laugh'd in his face ; and when with grief he wept,
    The ruthless Queen gave him to dry his cheeks
    A napkin steeped in the harmless blood
    Of sweet young Rutland, by rough Clifford slain .

5   And after many scorns, many foul taunts,
    They took his head, and on the gates of York
    They set the same, and there it doth remain,
    The saddest spectacle that e'er I view'd .

Messenger

1　　{†} {T}he Noble Duke of Yorke {is} slaine,
　　　Your Princely Father, and my loving Lord .

2　　Environed he was with many foes,
　　　And stood against them, as the hope of Troy
　　　Against the Greekes, that would have entred Troy .

3　　But Hercules himselfe must yeeld to oddes :
　　　And many stroakes, though with a little Axe,
　　　Hewes downe and fells the hardest-tymber'd Oake .

4　　By many hands your Father was subdu'd,
　　　But onely slaught'red by the irefull Arme
　　　Of un-relenting Clifford, and the Queene :
　　　Who crown'd the gracious Duke in high despight,
　　　Laugh'd in his face : and when with griefe he wept,
　　　The ruthlesse Queene gave him, to dry his Cheekes,
　　　A Napkin, steeped in the harmelesse blood
　　　Of sweet young Rutland, by rough Clifford slaine :
　　　And after many scornes, many foule taunts,
　　　They tooke his Head, and on the Gates of Yorke
　　　They set the same, and there it doth remaine,
　　　The saddest spectacle that ere I view'd .

- the two surround phrases concisely sum up the message, both the highly emotional capture of the Duke of Yorke ' . But Hercules himselfe must yeeld oddes : ' and Margaret's utter contempt ' : Who crown'd the gracious Duke in high despight,/Laugh'd in his face : '

- at the start (F #1-2) s/he stays in full control (9/3 in five lines), but already the first of the five extra breath-thoughts is seen in line 2, suggesting the need for an extra breath for both clarity and self-control

- as the capture of the Duke is first mentioned, the Messenger's personal feelings swamp the previously seen intellect (F #3, 3/8 in three lines!)

- and as the Messenger expands on the capture of Yorke; on Margaret's offering him the blood of his youngest son; and of Yorke's beheading, the F speech ends in one onrushed 12 line passionate sentence (13/15 up until its last two lines), suggesting the loss of objectivity – a loss most modern texts spoil by splitting the sentence in two: while grammatically correct, modern texts' rewrite essentially supports just the reporting the details of Yorke's death (the first sentence mt. #4), and his beheading (mt. #5); F's onrush seems to highlight the effects of the event on the Messenger as well

The Third Part of Henry the Sixt

Richard

I cannot weepe : for all my bodies moysture
between 2.1.79–88

Background: this is Richard's response to the news of the death of his father (prior speech).

Style: as part of a four-handed scene in front of a larger group

Where: in the open in Herefordshire

To Whom: his brothers Edward and George, in front of their forces, and the Messenger

# of Lines: 10

Probable Timing: 0.35 minutes

Take Note: Though the sentence structures of both texts match, F's orthography gives the lie to Richard's apparent self-control.

Richard

1   I cannot weep ; for all my body's moisture
    Scarce serves to quench my Furnace-burning [heart] ;
    Nor can my tongue unload my heart's great burthen,
    For self -same wind that I should speak withal
    Is kindling coals that fires all my breast ,
    And burns me up with flames that tears would quench .

2   To weep is to make less the depth of grief :
    Tears then for babes ; blows and revenge for me .

3   Richard, I bear thy name, I'll venge thy death,
    Or die renowned by attempting it .

Richard

1   I cannot weepe : for all my bodies moysture
     Scarse serves to quench my Furnace-burning [hart]:
     Nor can my tongue unloade my hearts great burthen,
     For selfe-same winde that I should speake withall,
     Is kindling coales that fires all my brest,
     And burnes me up with flames, that tears would quench .

2   To weepe, is to make lesse the depth of greefe :
     Teares then for Babes ; Blowes, and Revenge for mee .

3   Richard, I beare thy name, Ile venge thy death,
     Or dye renowned by attempting it .

- despite the repeated surround phrase claims that crying is weak

  " . I cannot weepe : for all my bodies moysture/Scarse serves to quench my Furnace-burning heart : ", and

  " : Teares then for Babes; Blowes, and revenge for mee . "

  F #1 and all but the last phrase of #2 are simply swamped with personal feelings (2/14 in just seven and a half lines), and the last two surround phrases contain a tell-tale (emotional) semicolon

- and even though some control is established for the last two and half lines of the speech, it is still (naturally) suffused with passion (3/4)

The Third Part of Henry the Sixt
Edward

A wispe of straw were worth a thousand Crowns,
2.2.144–162 & 126–128

Background: an agreement was made between the weak Lancastrian King Henry and his Yorkist rivals that the Duke of Yorke will take over the throne once Henry is dead. Despite this, Yorke's three adult sons have persuaded him to renege and continue the civil war for immediate possession of the English crown. Margaret, Henry's fierce wife and de facto leader of the Lancastrian forces, was eager to engage in combat, and in a previous skirmish has killed both Yorke and his youngest son, Rutland. The following, spoken by Yorke's oldest son, stems from a preliminary meeting between antagonists outside the town of York prior to another bloody battle. One note: to provide a 'tag' to the speech, part of an earlier demand from Edward has been used to create the last three lines.

Style: direct address essentially to two people in front of a larger group

Where: outside the town of York

To Whom: Margaret, and finally Henry, in front of the leaders both of Lancaster (including Clifford, Northumberland, and the young Prince of Wales) and Yorke (including brothers George and Richard, Warwicke, Norfolke, and Montague)

# of Lines: 22

Probable Timing: 1.10 minutes

Edward

1   A wisp of straw were worth a thousand crowns
     To make this shameless callet know her self .

2   Helen of Greece was fairer far [than] thou,
     Although thy husband may be Menelaus ;
     And ne'er was Agamemnon's brother wrong'd
     By that false woman as this king by thee .

3   His father revell'd in the heart of France,
     And tam'd the King, and made the Dolphin stoop ;
     And had he match'd according to his state,
     He might have kept that glory to this day .

4   But when he took a beggar to his bed,
     And grac'd thy poor sire with his bridal day,
     Even then that sunshine brew'd a show'r for him,
     That wash'd his father's fortunes forth of France,
     And heap'd sedition on his crown at home .

5   For what hath broach'd this tumult but thy pride?

6   Had'st thou been meek , our title still had slept,
     And we, in pity of the gentle king,
     Had slipt our claim until another age .

---

7   {2 sections   Say, Henry, shall I have my right, or no ?
     reversed}
8   A thousand men have broke their fasts to-day,
     That ne're shall dine unless thou yield the crown .

Edward

1   A wispe of straw were worth a thousand Crowns,
    To make this shamelesse Callet know her selfe :
    Helen of Greece was fayrer farre [then] thou,
    Although thy Husband may be Menelaus ;
    And ne're was Agamemnons Brother wrong'd
    By that false Woman, as this King by thee .

2   His Father revel'd in the heart of France,
    And tam'd the King, and made the Dolphin stoope :
    And had he match'd according to his State,
    He might have kept that glory to this day .

3   But when he tooke a begger to his bed,
    And grac'd thy poore Sire with his Bridall day,
    Even then that Sun-shine brew'd a showre for him,
    That washt his Fathers fortunes forth of France,
    And heap'd sedition on his Crowne at home :
    For what hath broach'd this tumult but thy Pride?

4   Had'st thou bene meeke, our Title still had slept,
    And we in pitty of the Gentle King,
    Had slipt our Claime, untill another Age .

---

5 {2 sections   Say Henry, shall I have my right, or no :
   reversed}   A thousand men have broke their Fasts to day,
    That ne're shall dine, unlesse thou yeeld the Crowne .

Take Note: F's orthography and sentence structure add more human details to Edward's belittling of Margaret before demanding the throne.

- basically the speech seems well under control, with capitals outweighing long spellings by almost two to one (30/18)

- the three extra breath-thoughts, especially in F #4-5, add to Yorke's occasional need to spell out his points in tiniest detail

- however, the onrush of both F's long sentences #1 and #3 suggests that the speech is not as grammatically controlled as Yorke would like (most modern texts split both F sentences into two)

- also, in two places (both directly insulting Margaret) passion seems to break through: this can be seen in the first four lines of F #1, a dig at her supposed beauty (6/5) and the three lines of F #5, essentially a slap at over-extending herself and playing the role of warrior instead of the traditional weaker female—3/3

- the surround phrases clearly establish Yorke's argument

    " : Helen of Greece were fayrer farre than thou, /Although thy husband may be Menelaus ; "

(the attack on Margaret's cuckolding of Henry is emphasized by finishing this attack with the only (emotional) semicolon in the speech), and

    " : For what hath broach'd this tumult but thy Pride ? ")

- and the surround phrase demanding that the kingdom be turned over to him

    " . Say Henry, shall I have my right, or no : "

is doubly enhanced, being both monosyllabic and, apart from the use of Henry's name, totally un-embellished—both clear signs that verbal games are at an end and now the basic core of the issue must be faced

The Third Part of Henry the Sixt
Son/Sonne

Ill blowes the winde that profits no body,
2.5.55 - 72

Background: whether the following speeches are figments of Henry's tortured imagination or actual events, the pain of discovery for each character is palpable in the extreme. Both speeches are the only ones for each character, and as such they are self explanatory.

Style: each solo

Where: close to the battlefield in Yorkshire

To Whom: a dead body, self, and direct audience address

# of Lines: 18

Probable Timing: 0.55 minutes

Take Note: The extra commas ending the opening two F lines suggest an onrolling sentence probably supporting the physical activity of dragging the body of the man he has just killed. Similarly, F allows the tremendous shock of discovering it is his father that he has killed due weight by setting the two unusually short sentences #2-3. Modern texts seem to mute both events by splitting F1 in two, and setting F #3 as the start of a new sentence, mt. #4.

Son

1 Ill blows the wind that profits nobody.

2 This man whom hand to hand I slew in fight
May be possessed with some store of crowns,
And I that, haply, take them from him now,
May yet, ere night, yield both my life and them
To some man else, as this dead man doth me .

3 Who's this?

4   O God ! it is my father's face,
Whom in this conflict I, unwares, have kill'd .

5 O heavy times ! begetting such events !

6 From London by the King was I press'd forth,
My father, being the Earl of Warwick's man,
Came on the part of York, press'd by his master ;
And I, who at his hands receiv'd my life,
Have by my hands, of life bereaved him .

7 Pardon me, God, I knew not what I did !
And pardon father, for I knew not thee !

8 My tears shall wipe away these bloody marks;
And no more words till they have flow'd their fill .

Sonne

1   Ill blowes the winde that profits no body,
    This man whom hand to hand I slew in fight,
    May be possessed with some store of Crownes,
    And I that (haply) take them from him now,
    May yet (ere night) yeeld both my Life and them
    To some man else, as this dead man doth me .

2   Who's this?

3   Oh God !

4   It is my Fathers face,
    Whom in this Conflict, I (unwares) have kill'd :
    Oh heavy times ! begetting such Events .

5   From London, by the King was I prest forth,
    My Father being the Earle of Warwickes man,
    Came on the part of Yorke, prest by his Master :
    And I, who at his hands receiv'd my life,
    Have by my hands, of Life bereaved him .

6   Pardon me God, I knew not what I did :
    And pardon Father, for I knew not thee .

7   My Teares shall wipe away these bloody markes :
    And no more words, till they have flow'd their fill .

- from the moment of discovery, the speech can be summed up by the first surround phrase with its very rare exclamation mark

  " : Oh heavy times ! Begetting such Events . "

  while the devastating effect on the Son is marked by the four successive surround phrases that end the speech

  " . Pardon me God, I knew not what I did:/ And pardon me Father, for I knew not thee . / My Teares shall wipe away these bloody markes : / And no more words, till they have flow'd their fill . "

- even after the emotional first line (0/2), the speech shows little intellectual energy, till the discovery of the identity of the dead man, perhaps suggesting that the battle had taken much out of the character (2/4 in six and a half lines, F #1-2)

- but once the discovery is made, surprisingly, intellect rather than passion freely flows (perhaps suggesting that the character is too stunned to fully emote (F #3-5, 12/5)

- the apology to God and his father is purely intellectual (2/0)

- and, while the opening of the final sentence is both intellectual and emotional (1/2), the last line is icy calm, as if finally everything is leached out of him

The Third Part of
Henry the Sixt
King {Henry}

O pitteous spectacle ! O bloody Times !
between 2.5.73 - 124

Background: the following is Henry's response to the prior speeches of Son and Father,

Style: solo

Where: close to the battlefield in Yorkshire

To Whom: self, and direct audience address

# of Lines: 19

Probable Timing: 1.00 minutes

Take Note: The large amount of major punctuation (7 colons and two semicolons, a very large number for such a short speech) suggest that Henry's brain is working overtime. Indeed, the long sentence F #4, split into six separate sentences in most modern texts, suggests that this is the first of what could be described as an overload/brain-storm/breakdown.

King

1   O piteous spectacle !

2   O bloody times !

3   Whiles lions war and battle for their dens,
     Poor harmless lambs abide their enmity .

4   Weep, wretched man : I'll aid thee tear for tear,
     And let our hearts and eyes, like civil war,
     Be blind with tears, and break o'ercharg'd with grief .

---

5   Woe above woe! grief , more [than] common grief !

6   O that my death would stay these ruthful deeds !

7   O, pity, pity, gentle heaven, pity!

8   The red rose and the white are on his face,
     The fatal colors of our striving houses ;
     The one his purple blood right well resembles,
     The other his pale cheeks, methinks, presenteth .

9   Wither one rose, and let the other flourish :
     If you contend, a thousand lives must wither .

---

10   Was ever king so griev'd for subjects' woe?

11   Much is your sorrow ; mine ten times so much .

---

12   Sad-hearted-men, much overgone with care,
     Here sits a King more woeful [than] you are .

King

1   O pitteous spectacle !

2   O bloody Times !

3   Whiles Lyons Warre, and battaile for their Dennes,
    Poore harmlesse Lambes abide their enmity .

4   Weepe wretched man : Ile ayde thee Teare for Teare,
    And let our hearts and eyes, like Civill Warre,
    Be blinde with teares, and break ore-charg'd with griefe

Wo above wo :greefe, more [thé] common greefe
O that my death would stay these ruthfull deeds :
O pitty, pitty, gentle heaven pitty :
The Red Rose and the White are on his face,
The fatall Colours of our striving Houses :
The one, his purple Blood right well resembles,
The other his pale Cheekes (me thinkes) presenteth :
Wither one Rose, and let the other flourish :
If you contend, a thousand lives must wither .

---

5   Was ever King so greev'd for Subjects woe?

6   Much is your sorrow ; Mine, ten times so much .

7   Sad-hearted-men, much overgone with Care ;
    Heere sits a King, more wofull [then] you are .

- the large number of surround phrases thus created are testament for the pain he feels he caused in others coming back to haunt him – the opening of F #4, the whole of F #7 and #8, plus those contained in the anguished onrush of F #5

   " : O pitty, pitty, gentle heaven pitty ; "

   and referring to the rose symbols of Yorke (white) and Lancaster (red)

   " : Wither one Rose, and let the other flourish ; /If you contend, a thousand lives must wither. "

- though his mind is working in the opening three F sentences and first three lines of F #4 (8 capitals in the six lines), his emotions are already swamping him, especially with the verbal weight of the long spellings (18 in all) emphasising the beginning or the end of a phrase or idea

- then, in F #4's next three lines, feelings take over completely (0/6)

- but, as he sees the symbol of the guilt of the two rival houses in the blood and death-mask of the dead son, so his intellect takes over for the rest of the speech (the remainder of F #4 through to #6, 11/5) by F #7, with the two unusually short sentences preceding it, and with the logical colons found in the middle of the speech now giving way to two (emotional) semicolons, it seems that Henry is finally subsumed by his woe, with the dry intellect of the penultimate line (1/0) and the final, emotional semicolon led, single line self-description (1/2)

The Tragedy of Richard the Third
Richard

{Brother Edward} cannot live I hope, and must not dye,
1.1.145–162

Background: the following is triggered by the wonderful news, for Richard, that 'The King is sickly, weake, and melancholly,/And his Physitians feare him mightily'. And, with elder brother King Edward so sick, the need to set a wedge between Edward and the second brother Clarence becomes even more urgent.

Style: solo

Where: unspecified, presumably a street near the palace

To Whom: direct address

# of Lines: 18

Probable Timing: 0.55 minutes

Take Note: The eight extra breath-thoughts scattered throughout the eighteen lines of the speech are just one sign of how specific Richard can be in planning and presentation.

Richard

1 {Brother Edward} cannot live, I hope, and must not die
   Till George be pack'd with post-horse up to heaven .

2 I'll in, to urge his hatred more to Clarence
   With lies well steel'd with weighty arguments,
   And if I fail not in my deep intent,
   Clarence hath not another day to live :
   Which done, God take King Edward to his mercy,
   And leave the world for me to bustle in !

3 For then I'll marry Warwick's youngest daughter .

4 What though I kill'd her husband and her father ?
   The readiest way to make the wench amends
   Is to become her husband, and her father :
   The which will I, not all so much for love
   As for another secret close intent
   By marrying her which I must reach unto .

5 But yet I run before my horse to market :
   Clarence still breathes, Edward still lives and reigns ,
   When they are gone, then must I count my gains .

Richard

1 {Brother Edward} cannot live I hope, and must not dye,
   Till George be pack'd with post-horse up to Heaven .

2 Ile in to urge his hatred more to Clarence,
   With Lyes well steel'd with weighty Arguments,
   And if I faile not in my deepe intent,
   Clarence hath not another day to live :
   Which done, God take King Edward to his mercy,
   And leave the world for me to bussle in .

3 For then, Ile marry Warwickes yongest daughter .

4 What though I kill'd her Husband, and her Father,
   The readiest way to make the Wench amends,
   Is to become her Husband, and her Father :
   The which will I, not all so much for love,
   As for another secret close intent,
   By marrying her, which I must reach unto .

5 But yet I run before my horse to Market :
   Clarence still breathes, Edward still lives and raignes,
   When they are gone, then must I count my gaines .

- the surround phrase shows how well he understands he is going to have to be patient

  " . But yet I run before my horse to Market : "

- though the speech is predominantly intellectual (including the opening 'Brother', 17/8 throughout), as are most of Richard's speeches in the early part of the play, at times he is remarkably careful, as with the non-embellished three lines ending F #4 with the (dreadful yet macabre) matter of fact dismissal of the reasons for marrying Lady Anne (whose immediate family he has already slaughtered): and even before this calm, the importance of marrying Anne is heralded by Richard via a very short sentence (F #3)

- elsewhere, the speech shifts between intellect and passion

  a. F #1, about Edward's eventual death, is intellectual (3/1)

  b. F #2, about Clarence's almost immediate demise, shifts to passion (4/3 until the colon)

  c. then Edward's subsequent death is once more treated intellectually (the last two lines of F #2), as is Richard's plan to marry Anne (F #3 and the first four lines of F #4, 9/1)

  d. then comes the already discussed three non-embellished lines ending F #4, hinting at the deeper reasons for the marriage

  e. and the final realisation that there is much to do (F #5) ends in passion (2/2)

The Tragedy of Richard the Third
Richard

I do the wrong, and first begin to brawle .
1.3.323–340

Background: again a self-explanatory speech, almost a quick check-in as to how the plotting against not just brother Clarence but now the Queen (brother Edward's wife) and her powerful family is progressing. The following is a quick aside between the exit of the family, badly shaken by a ferocious verbal attack upon them by the Lancastrian ex-Queen Margaret, and the entry of the men Richard has employed to kill Clarence.

Style: solo

Where: unspecified, presumably the palace

To Whom: direct address

# of Lines: 18

Probable Timing: 0.55 minutes

Take Note: While the sentence structures match, F's short opening suggests that Richard is absolutely naked in his celebration, but, after that, his passion begins to break through, at least while he is alone. And with no surround phrases and just one colon, the mind play seems more celebratory than purely intellectual.

Richard

1   I do the wrong, and first begin to brawl .

2   The secret mischiefs that I set abroach,
I lay unto the grievous charge of others .

3   Clarence, [whom] I indeed have cast in darkness ,
I do beweep to many simple gulls -
Namely to Derby, Hastings, Buckingham -
And tell them 'tis the Queen and her allies
That stir the King against the Duke my brother .

4   Now they believe it, and withal whet me
To be reveng'd on Rivers, Dorset, Grey .

5   But then I sigh, and, with a piece of scripture,
Tell them that God bids us do good for evil :
And thus I clothe my naked villainy
With odd old ends, stol'n forth of holy writ,
And seem a saint, when most I play the devil .

ENTER TWO MURTHERERS

6   But soft, here come my executioners.
How now my hardy, stout, resolved mates,
Are you now going to dispatch this thing ?

Richard

1   I do the wrong, and first begin to brawle .

2   The secret Mischeefes that I set abroach,
     I lay unto the greevous charge of others .

3   Clarence, [who] I indeede have cast in darknesse,
     I do beweepe to many simple Gulles,
     Namely to Derby, Hastings, Buckingham,
     And tell them 'tis the Queene, and her Allies,
     That stirre the King against the Duke my Brother .

4   Now they beleeve it, and withall whet me
     To be reveng'd on Rivers, Dorset, Grey .

5   But then I sigh, and with a peece of Scripture,
     Tell them that God bids us do good for evill :
     And thus I cloath my naked Villainie
     With odde old ends, stolne forth of holy Writ,
     And seeme a Saint, when most I play the devill .

ENTER TWO MURTHERERS

6   But soft, heere come my Executioners,
     How now my hardy stout resolved Mates,
     Are you now going to dispatch this thing ?

- for some reason it seems that Richard is holding himself in check in the first two F sentences as he begins to give voice to how well his plots are developing (disbelief? amazement? or even calm acceptance?), for F #1's very short opening, underscoring the double standard method of attack he is so successfully employing, is only slightly emotional (0/1), and F #2 only slightly passionate (1/2)

- but as he begins to detail his successes, so the restraint dissolves

  a. starting with the generality of Clarence (the first two lines of F #3) passion breaks through (1/4)

  b. which then quickly turns to a mental release as he describes how he has shifted the blame for Clarence's imprisonment onto the Queene and her family (a startling 8/2 in the last three lines of F #3)

- then the shifts in release become quicker and more marked, perhaps suggesting that in his delight his sense of self-control is somewhat slipping, for the joy of having seduced so many (F #4) quickly shifts from an emotional first line (0/2) back to an intellectual second as he lists whom his supporters also urge him to pull down (3/0)

- which leads to passion as he describes how he masks his 'Villanie' with his 'holy Writ' religious play-acting (5/6, F #5)

- but, once the Murtherers enter (F #6), one can almost see Richard putting a lid on his previous exuberance, moving from a passionate first line (1/1), to an intellectual second (1/0), to an ice-cold, non-embellished final question as to whether they are on their way to dispatch Clarence

The Tragedy of Richard the Third
Rivers

Sir Richard Ratcliffe, let me tell thee this,
between 3.3.2–26

Background: Ratcliffe is one of Richard's chief factotums, and as such he has been entrusted with the execution of three of Richard's perceived enemies—Rivers, the Queen's brother; Gray, one of her two sons from a previous marriage; and Sir Thomas Vaughn. This is a final speech before death, created for one character from words originally written for all three.

Style: part of a four-handed scene

Where: Pomfret Castle (in Yorkshire)

To Whom: Catesby, in front of his fellow prisoners condemned to death—his nephew Gray and colleague Sir Thomas Vaughn

# of Lines: 20

Probable Timing: 1.00 minutes

Take Note: F's orthography and sentence structure gently underscore the cracks in River's dignified last moments on earth.

Rivers

1 Sir Richard Ratcliffe, let me tell thee this :
  To-day shalt thou behold a subject die,
  For truth, for duty , and for loyalty .

2 O Pomfret, Pomfret !

3   O thou bloody prison !
  Fatal and ominous to noble peers !

4 Within the guilty closure of thy walls
  Richard the Second here was hack'd to death ;
  And for more slander to thy dismal seat,
  We give to thee our guiltless blood to drink .

5 {·} Now Margaret's curse is fall'n upon our heads,
  When she exclaim'd on Hastings, you, and I,
  For standing by when Richard stabb'd her son .

6 Then curs'd she Richard, then curs'd she Buckingham,
  Then curs'd she Hastings .

         Then curs'd she Hastings .

7 O , remember, God,
  To hear her prayer for them, as now for us!

8 And for my sister, and her princely sons ,
  Be satisfied , dear God, with our true blood,
  Which, as thou know'st, unjustly must be spilt .

9 Come, Grey, come, Vaughan, let us here embrace .

10 Farewell, until we meet again in heaven .

Rivers

1 Sir Richard Ratcliffe, let me tell thee this,
   To day shalt thou behold a Subject die,
   For Truth, for Dutie, and for Loyaltie .

2 O Pomfret, Pomfret !

3   O thou bloody Prison !
   Fatall and ominous to Noble Peeres :
   Within the guiltie Closure of thy Walls,
   Richard the Second here was hackt to death :
   And for more slander to thy dismall Seat,
   Wee give to thee our guiltlesse blood to drinke .

4 {*} Now Margarets Curse is falne upon our Heads,
   When shee exclaim'd on Hastings, you, and I,
   For standing by, when Richard stab'd her Sonne .

5 Then curs'd shee Richard,
   Then curs'd shee Buckingham,
   Then curs'd shee Hastings .

6 Oh remember God,
   To heare her prayer for them, as now for us :
   And for my Sister, and her Princely Sonnes,
   Be satisfy'd, deare God, with our true blood,
   Which, as thou know'st, unjustly must be spilt .

7 Come Grey, come Vaughan, let us here embrace .

8 Farewell, untill we meet againe in Heaven .

- there is an enormous dignity to the intellectual start by a man about to be unjustly executed (6/0, F #1), spoken to his executioner, possibly heightened by the (careful?) short spellings of 'Dutie' amd 'Loyaltie'

- the intellect continues into Rivers' address to the prison where he is about to die (10/3 in five lines, F #2 up to all but the last line of F #3)

- but the two longer sentences F #3 and #6, both of which most modern texts split in two, suggest that dignity might be more difficult to sustain than would at first appear

- for there is strain underneath, as evidenced by the very short F #2, and the sudden switch at the end of F #3 into pure emotion as the innocence of all three who are about to die is voiced (0/3 in just one line)

- the memory of Margaret's prophecy that they would die unnaturally brings back a strongly intellectual recollection (6/2 in F #4)

- which is somewhat undermined by
  a. the following sentence starting with an awkward split line, as if he were having difficulty in speaking
  b. the fact he suddenly becomes passionate in both the recollection and the appeal to God to extend their fate to Richard and his allies and protect his own family (8/7, the six lines of F #5-6)

- again, while it seems he has regained intellectual control as he turns to his comrades in death (F #7, 2/0), the fact that it and the final sentence are unusually short one line sentences again indicates the strain he is undergoing to maintain dignity

- and indeed, in the last sentence act of farewell passion creeps in once more (1/2)

The Tragedy of Richard the Third
Richard

Come hither Catesby, rumor it abroad,
4.2.50–66

Background: though still married to Lady Anne, Richard, as he explains in this speech, needs better familial and political connections than she can provide to justify his holding the throne. Two notes; 'Clarence Daughter' (line #5) and the 'Boy' (line #6) are references to the children of his older brother George who, since George's death, nominally are ahead of him in line for the throne—the assessment and action herein planned will effectively defuse their claims; 'Tyrrel', in the last line of the speech, is the man by whom Richard plans to have the true claimants to the crown, his oldest brother Edward's children, murdered (the famous 'Princes in the Tower').

Style: initially as part of a two-handed scene, then solo

Where: the palace

To Whom: at first to Catesby, his expediter of all matters, pleasant or otherwise, and then direct audience address

# of Lines: 17

Probable Timing: 0.55 minutes

Take Note: Not only does the F speech move faster than its modern counterpart, its orthography marks Richard's mood swings as both quick and violent.

Richard

1   Come hither, Catesby .

2   Rumor it abroad
That Anne my wife is very grievous sick ;
I will take order for her keeping close .

3   Inquire me out some mean poor gentleman,
Whom I will marry straight to Clarence daughter ;
The boy is foolish, and I fear not him .

4   Look how thou dream'st !

5   I say again , give out,
That Anne, my queen , is sick and like to die .

6   About it, for it stands me much upon
To stop all hopes whose growth may damage me .

7   I must be married to my brother's daughter,
Or else my kingdom stands on brittle glass .

8   Murther her brothers and then marry her -
Uncertain way of gain !

9   But I am in
So far in blood that sin will pluck on sin .

10   Tear-falling pity dwells not in this eye .

ENTER TYRREL

11   Is thy name Tyrrel ?

Richard

1   Come hither Catesby, rumor it abroad,
    That Anne my Wife is very grievous sicke,
    I will take order for her keeping close .

2   Inquire me out some meane poore Gentleman,
    Whom I will marry straight to Clarence Daughter :
    The Boy is foolish, and I feare not him .

3   Looke how thou dream'st : I say againe, give out,
    That Anne, my Queene, is sicke, and like to dye .

4   About it, for it stands me much upon
    To stop all hopes, whose growth may dammage me .

5   I must be marryed to my Brothers Daughter,
    Or else my Kingdome stands on brittle Glasse :
    Murther her Brothers, and then marry her,
    Uncertaine way of gaine .

6   But I am in
    So farre in blood, that sinne will pluck on sinne,
    Teare-falling Pittie dwells not in this Eye .

ENTER TYRREL

7   Is thy Name Tyrrel ?

- that the enormity of how Richard is planning to dispose of Anne gives even the cynical Catesby a moment of shock can be found in Richard's short surround phrase of command ' . Looke how thou dream'st : '

- the speed of Richard's mind can be seen

  a. in the four separate occasions where F's onrushed sentences (#1, #3, #5 and #6) are each split into their two correct grammatical components by most modern texts

  b. by the two fast-link commas which join mt. #1-2 as F #1, and mt. #9-10 as F #6

- as Richard's mind quickly shifts from topic to topic, so patterns of release change too, thus

  a. the first two lines of F #1, dealing with the disposal of Anne, opens intellectually (3/1), then finishes with the ice-calm death-warrant statement "I will take order for her keeping close."

  b. a little more passion (4/3) creeps into the handling of Clarence's children (F #2)

  c. Richard then explodes emotionally into the second command to Catesby to deal with Anne (2/5 in the two lines of F #3)

- then, with the exception of the last phrase, an icy, highly dangerous calm descends once more as Richard commands Catesby yet again, hinting at the enormous need behind the order (the first line and a half of F #4)

- and whether F #5-6 are addressed to Catesby or to himself, Richard is suddenly on a passionate roll (7/10 in just six lines) as he plans to remarry incestuously

- which Richard is immediately able to reduce to intellectual control once Tyrrel, the proposed murderer of his nephews enters (F #7, 2/0)

The Tragedy of Richard the Third
Richard

As I entend to prosper, and repent :
4.4.397–417

Background: having failed in every other attempt at persuading Elizabeth to agree to his marrying his niece, her daughter, Richard finally resorts to bullying, threatening countrywide massacre and destruction if he does not get his way.

Style: part of a two-handed scene, perhaps in front of a small group

Where: unspecified, perhaps a street near the Tower, or at the palace

To Whom: ex-Queen Elizabeth, perhaps in front of Catesby and Richard's military 'traine'

# of Lines: 21

Probable Timing: 1.05 minutes

Take Note: The amazing amount of heavy punctuation, twelve in just twenty-one lines, and the fact that they create no fewer than eleven surround phrases, show this to be one of the most hard-working speeches that Richard has in the play, opening with much more control than the modern texts' (mt. #1-3) exclamation marks suggest.

Richard

1   As I intend to prosper and repent,
    So thrive I in my dangerous affairs
    Of hostile arms !

2   Myself , myself confound !

3   [God] and fortune bar me happy hours !
    Day, yield me not thy light, nor night, thy rest !

4   Be opposite all planets of good luck
    To my proceeding, if with dear heart's love,
    Immaculate devotion, holy thoughts,
    I tender not thy beauteous princely daughter !

5   In her consists my happiness and thine ;
    Without her, follows to myself and thee ;
    Herself , the land, and many a Christian soul ,
    Death, desolation, ruin , and decay .

6   It cannot be avoided but by this ;
    It will not be avoided , but by this .

7   Therefore, dear mother—I must call you so -
    Be the attorney of my love to her .

8   Plead what I will be, not what I have been ;
    Not my deserts, but what I will deserve .

9   Urge the necessity and state of times,
    And be not peevish- [fond] in great designs .

Richard

1   As I entend to prosper, and repent :
     So thrive I in my dangerous Affayres
     Of hostile Armes: My selfe, my selfe confound :
     [Heaven], and Fortune barre me happy houres :
     Day, yeeld me not thy light ; nor Night, thy rest .

2   Be opposite all Planets of good lucke
     To my proceeding, if with deere hearts love,
     Immaculate devotion, holy thoughts,
     I tender not thy beautious Princely daughter .

3   In her, consists my Happinesse, and thine :
     Without her, followes to my selfe, and thee ;
     Her selfe, the Land, and many a Christian soule,
     Death, Desolation, Ruine, and Decay :
     It cannot be avoyded, but by this :
     It will not be avoyded, but by this .

4   Therefore deare Mother (I must call you so)
     Be the Atturney of my love to her :
     Pleade what I will be, not what I have beene ;
     Not my deserts, but what I will deserve :
     Urge the Necessity and state of times,
     And be not peevish [found], in great Designes .

- F's sentence structure shows Richard in a state of onrush rather than the modern texts' control (F #1 = mt.#1-3; F #3 = mt. #5-6; F #4 = mt.#7-9)

- the surround phrases outline the spine of his relentless attack, witness the whole of the opening sentence of pure destructive intent

    " . As I entend to prosper, and repent : /So thrive I in my dangerous Affayres/Of hostile Armes : My selfe, my selfe confound : /[Heaven], and Fortune barre me happy houres : /Day, yeeld me not thy light ; nor Night, thy rest . "

    followed by his insistence on marrying Elizabeth's daughter

    " . In her, consists my Happinesse, and thine : /Without her, followes to my selfe, and thee ; "

    otherwise the destruction of the Christian world will ensue

    " : It cannot be avoyded, but by this : /It will not be avoyded, but by this . "

    and the instructions to Elizabeth as to how to woo for him

    " : Pleade what I will be, not what I have beene ; /Not my deserts, but what I will deserve : "

- the eight extra breath-thoughts are testimony again to how carefully he is spelling everything out, especially in F #3

- the speech is basically passionate throughout (16/21 overall), with two touches of emotional release (the opening two and closing two lines of F #3, 1/3 and 0/2 respectively), and the surround phrase appeal to ' : Pleade what I will be, not what I have beene ; ' heightened even more by an emotional semicolon

The Life and Death of King John
Robert

My gracious Liege, when that my father liv'd,
between 1.1.95–115

Background: Robert, the younger of two sons to the deceased Sir Robert Faulconbridge, is claiming to be Sir Robert's true heir, asserting that the older brother Philip is illegitimate. In front of King John and the open court, Robert attempts to prove his case.

Style: address to the King in full view and hearing of a larger group

Where: the palace

To Whom: King John, in front of John's mother Eleanor, the lords Pembroke, Essex and Salisbury, a 'Sheriffe', and his brother Philip Faulconbridge

# of Lines: 19

Probable Timing: 1.00 minutes

Take Note: F's long second sentence gives the clue that Robert is not as easy in the Court as most modern texts, that divide F #2 in six, suggest—hardly surprising since he is accusing his mother of immoral behaviour with the brother of the current king!

Robert

1　My gracious liege, when that my father liv'd,
　Your brother did employ my father much—

　And once dispatch'd him in an embassy
　To Germany, there with the Emperor
　To treat of high affairs touching that time .

2　Th'advantage of his absence took the King,
　And in the mean time sojourn'd at my father's ;
　Where how he did prevail I shame to speak .

3　But truth is truth .

4　　　　　　　　　　　Large lengths of seas and shores
　Between my father, and my mother lay,
　As I have heard my father speak himself ,
　When this same lusty gentleman was got .

5　Upon his death-bed he by will bequeath'd
　His lands to me, and took it on his death
　That this my mother's son was none of his ;
　And if he were, he came into the world
　Full fourteen weeks before the course of time .

6　Then, good my liege , let me have what is mine,
　My father's land, as was my father's will .

Robert

1 My gracious Liege, when that my father liv'd,
   Your brother did imploy my father much .

---

2 And once dispatch'd him in an Embassie
   To Germany, there with the Emperor
   To treat of high affaires touching that time :
   Th'advantage of his absence tooke the King,
   And in the meane time sojourn'd at my fathers ;
   Where how he did prevaile, I shame to speake :
   But truth is truth, large lengths of seas and shores
   Betweene my father, and my mother lay,
   As I have heard my father speake himselfe
   When this same lusty gentleman was got :
   Upon his death-bed he by will bequeath'd
   His lands to me, and tooke it on his death
   That this my mothers sonne was none of his ;
   And if he were, he came into the world
   Full fourteene weeks before the course of time :
   Then good my Liedge let me have what is mine,
   My fathers land, as was my fathers will .

- the onrush of F #2, while divided neatly into presentation points by the major punctuation, suggests that although Robert knows what he wants to say he is presenting it in one long fixated blurt rather than in clean and separate steps

- the awkward embarrassment behind the speech is neatly summed up in the only surround phrase, initiated by one of only two (already emotional) semicolons in the speech, ' ; Where how he did prevaile, I shame to speake : '

- the other semicolon also is related to his embarrassment, linking 'That this my mothers sonne was none of his ; And if he were…'

- the lack of presentational smarts can even be seen in the penultimate line where speed rather than courtesy may be the mark, for whereas modern texts add two syntactically correct extra comma, without them the demand of 'Then good my Liedge let me have what is mine' is quite startling if played as one uninterrupted line

- another sign that Robert is ill at ease can be seen in the orthography underlying his vocal presentation, for while the opening five lines setting up the facts of his father's absence are somewhat intellectual and circumspect (4/2) , the next twelve, dealing with the delicate matter of infidelity and illegitimacy are highly emotional (1/10), and decorum only returns for the penultimate line of request (1/1, both on the pleading-for-authoritative-intervention from John as 'Liedge') and the non-embellished final (enforced calm?) line summarising his request—'My fathers land, as was my fathers will.'

The Life and Death of King John
Austria

Upon thy cheeke lay I this zelous kisse,
between 2.1.19–36

Background: Arthur's deceased father Geffrey was the middle brother between the deceased English King, Richard Coeur de Lion, and the youngest brother John. With the natural death of the older brother, Arthur should be King, but his uncle John has stolen the throne from him, forcing Arthur and his mother Constance into exile. Seeking European help to rectify the situation, to face John in military action if necessary, Constance has succeeded in gathering France and Austria to her side. In the following, Lymoges, Duke of Austria, proclaims his support for Arthur before the disputed city of Angiers.

Style: public address to one person for the benefit of both the individual and the larger group

Where: outside Angiers

To Whom: Arthur, in front of Constance, King Philip, King Philip's son Lewis the Dolphin, and French forces

# of Lines: 15

Probable Timing: 0.50 minutes

Take Note: While the sentence structure of both texts match, once more F's orthography offers more understanding of the humanity of a character caught in a public address situation.

Austria

1   Upon thy cheek lay I this zealous kiss
As seal to this indenture of my love :
That to my home I will no more return
Till Angiers, and the right thou hast in France,
Together with that pale, that white-fac'd shore,
Whose foot spurns back the ocean's roaring tides
And coops from other lands her islanders ,
Even till that England, hedg'd in with the main ,
That water-walled bulwark , still secure
And confident from foreign purposes,
Even till that utmost corner of the west
Salute thee for her king ; till then, fair boy,
Will I not think of home, but follow arms .

2   The peace of heaven is theirs [that] lift their swords
In such a just and charitable war .

Austria

1   Upon thy cheeke lay I this zelous kisse,
     As seale to this indenture of my love :
     That to my home I will no more returne
     Till Angiers, and the right thou hast in France,
     Together with that pale, that white-fac'd shore,
     Whose foot spurnes backe the Oceans roaring tides,
     And coopes from other lands her Ilanders,
     Even till that England hedg'd in with the maine,
     That Water-walled Bulwarke, still secure
     And confident from forreine purposes,
     Even till that utmost corner of the West
     Salute thee for her King, till then faire boy
     Will I not thinke of home, but follow Armes .

---

2   The peace of heaven is theirs[ÿ] lift their swords
     In such a just and charitable warre .

- though a public address, it seems that it takes Austria a moment to get any sort of mental facility going, for the first three lines of welcome are emotional (0/4)

- and then, in the single line that relates the senior partner in the pro-Arthur alliance and the town they hope to take on his behalf (France and Angiers respectively), a flicker of intellect makes itself felt (2/0)

- and then, in the remaining nine lines of the braggadocio sentence, Austria hits his full passionate bombastic stride (8/9)

- F #2 becomes calmer (0/1 in two lines), as if in marrying France's reasons for the war to religion, 'the peace of heaven', has brought a sense of momentary dignity to the proceedings

The Life and Death of King John
Bastard

Go, beare him in thine armes :
4.3.139–159

Background: Arthur has died, not through foul play, but by falling off a high roof while trying to escape from his imprisonment. The discovery of the body is sufficient to push the already dubious nobles to join with French invasion forces and fight against John. Initially suspicious of Hubert's complicity in the child's death, the Bastard is now convinced of his innocence, and begins to plan with him how to deal with the current appalling situation.

Style: as part of a two-handed scene

Where: in a public street

To Whom: Hubert, in front of Arthur's body

# of Lines: 21

Probable Timing: 1.05 minutes

Take Note: The enormity of the death of the child throws Phillip (the 'Bastard', also referred to in the play as 'Sir Richard') into an emotional crisis in which his intellect does not necessarily have the answers, the struggle clearly seen in the onrush of four F sentences when compared to the modern texts, and the large-scale sweeps in vocal patterning.

Bastard

1 Go, bear him in thine arms .

2 I am amaz'd methinks , and lose my way
   Among the thorns and dangers of this world .

3 How easy dost thou take all England up

4 From forth this morsel of dead royalty !
   The life, the right, and truth of all this realm
   Is fled to heaven, and England now is left
   To tug and [scramble], and to part by th'teeth
   The unowed interest of proud swelling state .

5 Now for the bare-pick'd bone of majesty
   Doth dogged war bristle his angry crest,
   And snarleth in the gentle eye of peace ;
   Now powers from home, and discontents at home
   Meet in one line ; and vast confusion waits ,
   As doth a raven on a sick -fall'n beast,
   The imminent decay of wrested pomp .

6 Now happy he whose cloak and [ceintur e] can
   Hold out this tempest .

7   Bear away that child ,
   And follow me with speed .

8   I'll to the King .

9 A thousand businesses are brief in hand,
   And heaven itself doth frown upon the land !

Bastard

1   Go, beare him in thine armes :
I am amaz'd me thinkes, and loose my way
Among the thornes, and dangers of this world .

2   How easie dost thou take all England up,
From forth this morcell of dead Royaltie?

3   The life, the right, and truth of all this Realme
Is fled to heaven : and England now is left
To tug and [scamble], and to part by th'teeth
The un-owed interest of proud swelling State :
Now for the bare-pickt bone of Majesty,
Doth dogged warre bristle his angry crest,
And snarleth in the gentle eye of peace :
Now Powers from home, and discontents at home
Meet in one line : and vast confusion waites
As doth a Raven on a sicke-falne beast,
The iminent decay of wrested pompe .

4   Now happy he, whose cloake and [center] can
Hold out this tempest .

5   Beare away that childe,
And follow me with speed : Ile to the King :
A thousand businesses are briefe in hand,
And heaven it selfe doth frowne upon the Land .

- the surround phrases clearly outline his struggle, viz. ' . Go, beare him in thine armes : ' and ' . Beare away that childe,/And follow me with speed : Ile to the King : '

- F1's pure emotion (0/5) and onrush (reduced by most modern texts that split the sentence in two) show just how badly the bastard (Phillip) is shaken

- as originally set, F #2's two line sentence sets up the bleak thought of England inexorably tied up with the dead child, foreshadowing the bad times which Phillip then expands upon in the onrushed F #3: the rewrite of most modern texts simply equates Arthur as England (mt. #3), which leads the gloomy reflection of what they set as mt. #4-5 to come rather out of the blue—and by splitting the ugly future in two they make quite an intellectual analysis of it, whereas the longer eleven line F #3 suggests that Phillip simply cannot get the images out of his mind

- interestingly, F #2 and the opening eight and a half line gloom of F #3 are strongly intellectual (7/3), perhaps suggesting the modern rewrite might be better after all, but then in the last two and a half lines of F #3, when all the individual horrors become one general vast confusion, so the emotional wash that opened the speech sweeps in once more (1/4)

- and sadly, for such a once lively and opportunistic character, this emotional distress intensifies not just in F #4 but also in the last non-grammatical (according to most modern texts) onrushed F #5, which suggests that Phillip's lack of confidence is still weighing him down, unlike his modern counterpart who has been given three separate rational sentences by which to finish the scene

The Life and Death of King Richard the Second
Richard

Needs must I like it well :I weepe for joy
3.2.4–26

Background: in part with Gaunt's money, Richard has embarked
upon the Irish wars. Unfortunately, seizing Gaunt's money has
given the English malcontents a focussed leader, Gaunt's son (and
Richard's cousin) Bullingbrooke, who has made great gains in
Richard's absence, capturing and executing several of Richard's in-
timate circle, including Bushy and Greene. Richard has returned
from Ireland not yet knowing the full extent of the rebels' progress;
the following is triggered by Aumerle's question 'how brooks your
Grace the ayre,/after your late tossing on the breaking Seas?'.

Style: general address, as part of a three handed scene in front of a
larger group

Where: the Welsh coast near the castle variously described as
Barkloughly, Hertloughly, and Harlechly, near Harlech

To Whom: the earth and those accompanying him, Aumerle, the
bishop of Carlile, and soldiers

# of Lines: 23

Probable Timing: 1.10 minutes

Take Note: F's orthography shows where, how, and what is causing
Richard to fall apart.

Richard

1   Needs must I like it well ;I weep for joy
     To stand upon my kingdom once again .

2   Dear earth, I do salute thee with my hand,
     Though rebels wound thee with their horses' hoofs .

3   As a long parted mother with her child
     Plays fondly with her tears , and smiles in meeting,
     So weeping, smiling, greet I thee my earth,
     And do thee [favors] with my royal hands .

4   Feed not thy sovereign's foe, my gentle earth,
     Nor with thy sweets comfort his ravenous sense ,
     But let thy spiders, that suck up thy venom ,
     And heavy -gaited toads lie in their way,
     Doing annoyance to the treacherous feet ,
     Which with usurping steps do trample thee .

5   Yield stinging nettles to mine enemies ;
     And when they from thy bosom pluck a flower,
     Guard it, I [pray thee], with a lurking adder,
     Whose double tongue may with a mortal touch
     Throw death upon thy sovereign's enemies .

6   Mock not my senseless conjuration, lords,
     This earth shall have a feeling, and these stones
     Prove armed soldiers , ere her native king
     Shall falter under foul [rebellion's] arms .

Richard

1   Needs must I like it well : I weepe for joy
    To stand upon my Kingdome once againe .

2   Deere Earth, I doe salute thee with my hand,
    Though Rebels wound thee with their Horses hoofes :
    As a long parted Mother with her Child,
    Playes fondly with her teares, and smiles in meeting ;
    So weeping, smiling, greet I thee my Earth,
    And doe thee [favor] with my Royall hands .

3   Feed not thy Soveraignes Foe, my gentle Earth,
    Nor with thy Sweetes, comfort his ravenous sence :
    But let thy Spiders, that suck up thy Venome,
    And heavie-gated Toades lye in their way,
    Doing annoyance to the trecherous feete,
    Which with usurping steps doe trample thee .

4   Yeeld stinging Nettles to mine Enemies ;
    And when they from thy Bosome pluck a Flower,
    Guard it I [prethee] with a lurking Adder,
    Whose double tongue may with a mortall touch
    Throw death upon thy Soveraignes Enemies .

5   Mock not my sencelesse Conjuration, Lords ;
    This Earth shall have a feeling, and these Stones
    Prove armed Souldiers, ere her Native King
    Shall falter under foule [Rebellious] Armes .

- the three emotional semicolons underscore three strands that are beginning to pull Richard apart
  a. first, and perhaps most frighteningly, that he knows he is not thinking rationally, "Mock not my senceless Conjuration, Lords;"
  b. second, that he is emotionally very vulnerable, comparing himself to a mother 'long parted' with a child, one who 'Playes fondly with her teares, and smiles in meeting;'
  c. third, there is an extraordinarily violent well of anger in him toward Bullingbrooke and his allies, ' . Yeeld stinging Nettles to mine Enemies ; ', this last only one of two surround phrases in the speech

- Richard's sense of fatalism is underscored by the other surround phrase that opens the speech, ' . Needs must I like it well : ', especially since the phrase is both unembellished and monosyllabic

- the only rushed passage in the speech (F #2, versus mt. #2-3) suggests Richard's love for England (acknowledging how badly he may have used it for his own foolish pleasures), is very genuine, for the onrush where modern texts divide the sentence in two is where the thought of wounded England releases his tears

- after the first fatalistic phrase, the speech itself starts in emotion (and tears, 1/3 in the one and a half lines finishing F #1)

- F #2's onrushed greeting of the earth of England is passionate (7/7)

- F #3 hints at the struggles within him, for the two line passionate opening begging the earth not to aid his enemies (4/3) leads to the highly passionate two lines specifying the form the curse should take (3/3), and ends with the emotional two line wished for results (0/2)

- amazingly, by the end of the speech he manages to regain mental control over himself, slowly at first as he finishes the curse (7/4, F #4) and then more rapidly with the realisation that he is indulging himself in 'sencelesse' thoughts, (9/4)

The Life and Death of King Richard the Second
Richard

Discomfortable Cousin, knowest thou not,
3.2.36–63

Background: in the face of the growing support for Bullingbrooke's cause while Richard was in Ireland, supporters are attempting to strengthen Richard's resolve upon his return. The Bishop of Carlile is stressing the divine right of established kings, 'that Power that made you King/Hath power to keepe you King, in spight of all'. The more pragmatic Aumerle is not so easily persuaded, arguing that the Bishop's statement is not necessarily valuable or practical, 'He meanes my lord, that we are too remisse,/Whilest Bullingbrooke through our securitie,/Growes strong and great, in substance and in friends', which triggers the following.

Style: as part of a three handed scene, in front of a larger group

To Whom: to Aumerle, in front of the Bishop of Carlile and their forces

Where: the Welsh coast near the castle variously described as Barkloughly, Hertloughly, and Harlechly, near Harlech

# of Lines: 27

Probable Timing: 1.20 minutes

Take Note: Here, at probably the apex of Richard's belief in his own divine superiority, F presents a very confident man.

Richard

1   Discomfortable cousin, know'st thou not,
     That when the searching eye of heaven is hid
     Behind the globe, that lights the lower world,
     Then thieves and robbers range abroad unseen ,
     In murthers and in outrage [boldly] here,
     But when from under this terrestrial ball
     He fires the proud tops of the eastern pines,
     And darts his [light] through every guilty hole,
     Then murthers, treasons, and detested sins ,
     The cloak of night being pluck'd from off their backs,
     Stand bare and naked, trembling at themselves ?

2   So when this thief , this traitor Bullingbrook ,
     Who all this while hath revell'd in the night,
     [Whilst we were wand'ring with the antipodes,]
     Shall see us rising in our throne, the east,
     His treasons will sit blushing in his face,
     Not able to endure the sight of day,
     But self -affrighted, tremble at his sin .

3   Not all the water in the rough rude sea
     Can wash the balm [off] from an anointed king ;
     The breath of worldly men cannot depose
     The deputy elected by the Lord ;
     For every man that Bullingbrook hath press'd
     To lift shrewd steel against our golden crown ,
     [God] for his Richard hath in heavenly pay
     A glorious angel ;then if angels fight,
     Weak men must fall, for heaven still guards the right .

                    ENTER SALISBURY

4   Welcome, my lord .

5   How far off lies your power ?

Richard

1 Discomfortable Cousin, knowest thou not,
   That when the searching Eye of Heaven is hid
   Behind the Globe, that lights the lower World,
   Then Theeves and Robbers raunge abroad unseene,
   In Murthers and in Out-rage [bloody] here :
   But when from under this Terrestriall Ball
   He fires the prowd tops of the Easterne Pines,
   And darts his [Lightning] through ev'ry guiltie hole,
   Then Murthers, Treasons, and detested sinnes
   (The Cloake of Night being pluckt from off their backs)
   Stand bare and naked, trembling at themselves .

2 So when this Theefe, this Traytor Bullingbrooke,
   Who all this while hath revell'd in the Night,

                    ∞

   Shall see us rising in our Throne, the East,
   His Treasons will sit blushing in his face,
   Not able to endure the sight of Day ;
   But selfe-affrighted, tremble at his sinne .

3 Not all the Water in the rough rude Sea
   Can wash the Balme [ ]from an anoynted King ;
   The breath of worldly men cannot depose
   The Deputie elected by the Lord :
   For everyman that Bullingbrooke hath prest,
   To lift shrewd Steele against our Golden Crowne,
   [Heaven] for his Richard hath in heavenly pay
   A glorious Angell : then if Angels fight,
   Weake men must fall, for Heaven still guards the right .

ENTER SALISBURY

4 Welcome my Lord, how farre off lyes your Power ?

- Richard seems so utterly convinced of his invincibility, that, according to the surround phrases, at the sight of him in his full glory, the guilty will

  " ; But selfe-affrighted, tremble at his sinne . ",

  a belief intensified in part by an (emotional) semicolon, supported by the only non-embellished line in the speech predicting they will 'Stand bare and naked, trembling at themselves.', adding, via another surround phrase, besides

  " : then if Angels fight/Weake men must fall, for heaven still guards the right . "

  a belief unconsciously intensified by the use of the rhyming couplet

- much of this confidence seems to stem from his belief that he is divinely appointed, the second semicolon of the speech marking his absolute conviction that nothing could possibly 'wash the Balme from an anointed King;'

- this intellectual confidence runs right through the speech (42/23 overall), the one emotional moment being the first surround phrase ending F #2, discussed above

- though the mention of Bullingbrooke and his men brings a small emotional surge (5/4 following the penultimate colon in F #3) leading into the confident assumption that they will be matched by Angels fighting on Richard's own behalf

- even the mildly onrushed final sentence F #4, which most modern texts split in two, displays an ease and almost cavalier approach to what he believes will be a heavenly guided victory, and, interestingly enough, this is the only truly matching intellectual/emotional sentence in the speech (2/2)

The Life and Death of King Richard the Second
Richard

What must the King doe now ?must he submit ?
3.3.143–159

Background: Bullingbrooke has made no formal demands of Richard other than the 'scope/Then for his Lineall Royalties, and to begge/ Infrachisement immediate', yet despite this Richard immediately concludes the worst. This speech is spoken to his supporters once Northumberland has returned from Bullingbrooke, having conveyed to him Richard's agreement to accede to Bullingbrooke's familial reinstatement and pardon.

Style: small group address as part of a five handed scene

Where: on the walls at the castle near Harlech

To Whom: Aumerle, Bishop Carlile, Scroope, and Salisbury

# of Lines: 17

Probable Timing: 0.55 minutes

Take Note: The combination of the opening two short sentences (on-rushed according to most modern texts that split each into two); the eight surround phrases, especially the two ending the speech; the cluster of six extra breath-thoughts in the middle of the speech; and the single non-embellished line, are all testament to how much turmoil Richard is now going through, despite the apparent intellectualism of the speech (34/18 overall).

Richard

1   What must the King do now ?

2   Must he submit ?

3   The King shall do it .

4   Must he be depos'd ?

5   The King shall be contented .

6   Must he lose
The name of king ?[a]'Gods name let it go .

7   I'll give my jewels for a set of beads ,
My gorgeous palace for a hermitage,
My gay apparel for an alms man's gown ,
My figur'd goblets for a dish of wood,
My sceptre for a palmer's walking staff ,
My subjects for a pair of carved saints,
And my large kingdom for a little grave,
A little little grave, an obscure grave—
Or I'll be buried in the king's high way,
Some way of common trade, where subjects' feet
May hourly trample on their sovereign's head ;
For on my heart they tread now whilst I live,
And buried once, why not upon my head ?

Richard

1   What must the King doe now ?must he submit ?

2   The King shall doe it : Must he be depos'd ?

3   The King shall be contented : Must he loose
     The Name of King ?[o]'Gods Name let it goe .

4   Ile give my Jewels for a sett of Beades,
     My gorgeous Pallace, for a Hermitage,
     My gay Apparrell, for an Almes-mans Gowne,
     My figur'd Goblets, for a Dish of Wood,
     My Scepter, for a Palmers walking Staffe,
     My Subjects, for a payre of carved Saints,
     And my large Kingdome, for a little Grave,
     A little little Grave, an obscure Grave .

5   Or Ile be buryed in the Kings high-way,
     Some way of common Trade, where Subjects feet
     May howrely trample on their Soveraignes Head :
     For on my heart they tread now, whilest I live ;
     And buryed once, why not upon my Head ?

- the naked bluntness of the almost monosyllabic first line (1/1) going right to the unheard-of, unprecedented, heart of the problem, forced abdication, speaks volumes as to the seriousness of the opening, with Richard no longer spinning his usual complex passionate hyperbole

- the intellectual drive of the five surround phrases of the next two sentences (8/3 F #2-3) is essentially a more vehement onrushed repetition of F #1—onrushed in that most modern texts take the opening three F sentences and reset them as six, making the modern opening a series of demands for answers, whereas F seems to offer a mind-whirling acceptance of the situation

- then as the extra breath thoughts pour in from F #4 on, the purple imagery starts up once more, the extra commas qualifying even more everything he is envisaging losing, possessions and life: yet in the midst of the hyperbole his mind is still crystal-clear, even though until the last two lines dealing with death he may be concentrating too much on the mere trappings of a king (19/9)

- F #5, set as a separate sentence, suggests his preoccupation with death (see speech #14 above) and has tremendous importance for him, especially when the final two surround phrases ending the speech are taken into account: most modern texts reduce this importance by enfolding it into the sense of general loss that begins the long mt. #7

The Life and Death of King Richard the Second
Richard

Aumerle, thou weep'st (my tender-hearted Cousin)
between 3.3.160–183

Background: Bullingbrooke has made no formal demands of Richard other than the 'scope/Then for his Lineall Royalties, and to begge/ Infrachisement immediate', yet despite this Richard immediately concludes the worst. This speech is a direct continuation of the previous speech, but could be treated as a separate component.

Style: small group address as part of a five handed scene

Where: on the walls at the castle near Harlech

To Whom: Aumerle, Bishop Carlile, Scroope, and Salisbury

# of Lines: 22

Probable Timing: 1.10 minutes

Take Note: The only surround phrase, ' . In the base Court, come down : ', doubly weighted by being monosyllabic and starting as it does the last sentence of the speech, seems to suggest Richard is (consciously?) postponing the inevitable.

Richard

1 Aumerle, thou weep'st, my tender-hearted cousin !

2 We'll make foul weather with despised tears ;
   Our sighs and they shall lodge the summer corn ,
   And make a dearth in this revolting land .

3 Or shall we play the wantons with our woes
   And make some pretty match with shedding tears ?
   As thus to drop them still upon one place,
   Till they have fretted us a pair of graves
   Within the earth, and therein laid—there lies
   Two kinsmen digg'd their graves with weeping eyes ?

4 Would not this ill do well ?

5   Well, well, I see
   I talk but idlely , and you [laugh] at me .

6 Most mighty prince, my Lord Northumberland,
   What says King Bullingbrook ?

7   Will his Majesty
   Give Richard leave to live till Richard die?

8 You make a leg , and Bullingbrook says ay .

   Wanting the manage of unruly jades .

10 In the base court ?

11   Base court, where king's grow base,
    To come at traitors' calls and do them grace .

12 In the base court, come down .

13   Down court ! down king!
    For night-owls shriek where mounting larks should
                                              sing .

Richard

1 Aumerle, thou weep'st (my tender-hearted Cousin)
   Wee'le make foule Weather with despised Teares :
   Our sighes, and they, shall lodge the Summer Corne,
   And make a Dearth in this revolting Land .

2 Or shall we play the Wantons with our Woes,
   And make some prettie Match, with shedding Teares ?
   As thus : to drop them still upon one place,
   Till they have fretted us a payre of Graves,
   Within the Earth : and therein lay'd, there lyes
   Two Kinsmen, digg'd their Graves with weeping Eyes ?

3 Would not this ill, doe well ?

4   Well, well, I see
   I talke but idly, and you [mock] at mee .

5 Most mightie Prince, my Lord Northumberland,
   What sayes King Bullingbrooke ?

6   Will his Majestie
   Give Richard leave to live, till Richard die ?
   You make a Legge, and Bullingbrooke sayes I .

8 Downe, downe I come, like glist'ring Phaeton,
   Wanting the manage of unruly Jades .

9 In the base Court ? base Court, where Kings grow base,
   To come at Traytors Calls, and doe them Grace .

10 In the base Court come down : down Court, down King,
   For night-Owls shrike, where mounting Larks should
                                                    sing .

- before facing the real politick of Northumberland, Richard shares the emotion of the moment with Aumerle both with an onrushed F #1, and passion referring to their tears (3/3 in the opening two lines), which he intellectually suggests, through a stretched harvesting analogy, could ruin the land, or even dig them both a pair of graves (the last two lines of F #1 through to the end of F #2, 10/2)

- the onrush suggests that despite the mental gymnastics involved, self-control is still rather difficult, which is echoed by the six extra breath-thoughts to date, and a seventh coming in the very short sentence F #3, an emotional (0/1) pun

- his emotional dislike of the political onslaught Northumberland represents, together with his brilliant political assessing of it, can be seen in the passage of three short/semi-short sentences F #4-6, none longer than a line and a half

- the recognition that he is talking 'idly' is emotional (0/2, F #4)

- his overly fulsome flattery of his arch-nemesis Northumberland and blunt question as to whether Bullingbrooke will allow him to live, is relentlessly intellectual (8/2 in just three lines, F #5-6)

- Richard's understanding of the symbiotic relationship between Northumberland's action and Bullingbrooke's intent, and his ironic self-description as the charioteer who draws the sun-god (Phaeton, the charioteer who could not control his unruly beasts) rather than the sun-god himself, releases his passions (4/5, F #7-8)—the unruly beasts presumably a reference to the nobles ranged against him

- his final superlative, passive-aggressive, insulting word-play on the 'base' court and its ramifications is once more superbly intellectual (10/3 in just the four lines of F #9-10)

The Life and Death of King Richard the Second
Richard

Alack, why am I sent for to a King,
4.1.162–176

Background: though Richard has already sent a message agreeing to abdicate in favour of Bullingbrooke, Bullingbrooke has ordered 'Fetch hither Richard, that in common view/He may surrender: so shall we proceede/Without suspition'. Richard is brought in by his uncle Yorke, and this is his first of a series of potentially Bullingbrooke-embarrassing questions.

Style: general address to a large group

Where: the Parliament at Westminster

To Whom: Bullingbrooke, in front of Yorke, Northumberland, Harry Percie, Aumerle, Fitz-Water, Surrey, herald, officers, and two supporters of Richard, Bagot and the Bishop of Carlile

# of Lines: 15

Probable Timing: 0.45 minutes

Take Note: As with the ending of the previous speech, at key moments Richard seems very subdued, though not for long.

Richard

1   Alack, why am I sent for to a king
Before I have shook off the regal thoughts
Wherewith I reign'd?

2   I hardly yet have learn'd
To insinuate, flatter, bow, and bend my knee.

3   Give sorrow leave a while, to tutor me
To this submission.

4   Yet I well remember
The favors of these men.

5   Were they not mine?

6   Did they not [sometimes] cry, "All hail!" to me?

7   So Judas did to Christ :but He in twelve,
Found truth in all but one; I, in twelve thousand, none.

8   God save the King!

9   Will no man say amen?

10   Am I both priest and clerk?

11   Well then, amen.

12   God save the King! although I be not he,
And yet amen, if heaven do think him me.

13   To do what service am I sent for hither?

Richard

1　Alack, why am I sent for to a King,
　　Before I have shooke off the Regall thoughts
　　Wherewith I reign'd ?

2　　　　　　　　　　　　　I hardly yet have learn'd
　　To insinuate, flatter, bowe, and bend my Knee .

3　Give Sorrow leave a while, to tuture me
　　To this submission .

4　　　　　　　　　　Yet I well remember
　　The favors of these men :were they not mine ?

5　Did they not [sometime] cry, All hayle to me ?

6　So Judas did to Christ : but he in twelve,
　　Found truth in all, but one ; I, in twelve thousand, none .

7　God save the King : will no man say, Amen ?

8　Am I both Priest, and Clarke ? well then, Amen .

9　God save the King, although I be not hee :
　　And yet Amen, if Heaven doe thinke him mee .

10　To doe what service, am I sent for hither ?

- the passionate statement opening the speech, still asserting his status as a king, is passionate (4/4, F #1-3), even with the quiet non-embellished lines underscoring the new realities he has to face

   " I hardly yet have learn'd/To insinuate, flatter,"

- a quiet augmented by F #4's non-embellished surround phrases

   " . Yet I well remember /The favours of these men : were they not mine ? "

- however, with the remainder of the speech being composed either of short sentences and/or surround phrases, a new energy of intellectual protestation makes itself felt, firstly via another overweening piece of self-comparison with Christ ' : but he in twelve/Found truth in all, but one ; I in twelve thousand, none . ' (3/1, F #5-6)

- and in seemingly accepting his loss, and Bullingbrooke's ascent (F #7-8), the combination of two short sentences, four surround phrases, and two extra breath-thoughts all give rise initially to a continuation of the intellect and then, with no answer, a move to passionate word play at Bullingbrooke's expense (F #9, 3/4)

- however, the passive-aggressive energies disappear in the last (short) naked reality accepting sentence, 'To doe what service, am I sent for hither?', the extra breath-thought and final non-embellished phrase speaking volumes as to his true understanding of the situation

The Life and Death of King Richard the Second
Bullingbrooke

Exton, I thanke thee not, for thou hast wrought
between 5.6.34–52

Background: in an earlier scene Exton claims to have heard Bullingbrooke say 'Have I no friend will rid me of this living feare'. Exton
has taken Bullingbrooke (now King Henry IV) at his word, jour-
neyed to Yorkshire, killed Richard, and brought his body back to
Bullingbrooke as proof, and, presumably, for reward. The following
is Bullingbrooke's reply.

Style: one on one address in front of a larger group

Where: Windsor Castle

To Whom: Exton, in front of Yorke, Northumberland, Fitz-Water,
Harry Percie, Bishop of Carlile, and 'other lords'

# of Lines: 18

Probable Timing: 1.00 minutes

Take Note: Most of the seven extra breath-thoughts scattered through
the speech come at the moments when Bullingbrooke is expressing
sadness or regret or anger for Richard's death: these coupled with
F's two onrushed sentences (F #2 and #6) and the preponderance
of emotion throughout (8/15) suggest that the remorse expressed
in the speech may be quite genuine rather than a rhetorical ploy.
Bullingbrooke's opening passion (2/3, F #1) is accompanied by two
of the breath-thoughts, pointing out how Exton's action will black-
en his, Bullingbrooke's, name as well as the country

Bullingbrooke

1   Exton, I thank thee not, for thou hast wrought
    A deed of [slander], with thy fatal hand
    Upon my head and all this famous land .

---

2   They love not poison that do poison need ,
    Nor do I thee .

3   Though I did wish him dead,
    I hate the murtherer, love him murthered .

4   The guilt of conscience take thou for thy labor ,
    But neither my good word nor princely favor .

5   With Cain go wander through the [shades] of night,
    And never show thy head by day nor light .

6   Lords, I protest my soul is full of woe
    That blood should sprinkle me to make me grow .

7   Come mourn with me for [what] I do lament,
    And put on sullen black incontinent .

8   I'll make a voyage to the Holy Land,
    To wash this blood off from my guilty hand .

9   March sadly after, grace my [mournings] here ,
    In weeping after this untimely bier .

Bullingbrooke

1 Exton, I thanke thee not, for thou hast wrought
   A deede of [Slaughter], with thy fatall hand,
   Upon my head, and all this famous Land .

---

2 They love not poyson, that do poyson neede,
   Nor do I thee :though I did wish him dead,
   I hate the Murtherer, love him murthered .

3 The guilt of conscience take thou for thy labour,
   But neither my good word, nor Princely favour .

4 With Caine go wander through the [shade] of night,
   And never shew thy head by day, nor light .

5 Lords, I protest my soule is full of woe,
   That blood should sprinkle me, to make me grow .

6 Come mourne with me, for [that] I do lament,
   And put on sullen Blacke incontinent :
   Ile make a voyage to the Holy-land,
   To wash this blood off from my guilty hand .

7 March sadly after, grace my [mourning] heere,
   In weeping after this untimely Beere .

- F #2's attack to Exton seems both fervent (being made up of surround phrases) and emotional, with a one and a half line surround phrase (0/3) opening the attack

  " . They love not poyson, that do poyson neede,/Nor do I thee : "

  being quickly followed by an unequivocal intellectual follow up (1/0)

  " : though I did wish him dead,/I hate the Murtherer, love him murthered . "

- one emotional line should be noted, 'Lords, I protest my soule is full of woe,' (0/3), especially since it is followed by the extra breath thought leading to the second non-embellished line discussed below, that line also magnified by an extra breath thought

- while the rest of the speech remains more emotional than intellectual-passionate (5/9 in the remaining twelve lines), following the non-embellished line banishing Exton

  "And never shew thy head by day, nor light."

  the two other non-embellished lines might suggest that Bullingbrooke is somewhat fixated on the blood that has been spilled, lamenting

  "That blood should sprinkle me, to make me grow."

  and vowing to go on a Crusade

  "To wash this blood off from my guilty hand."

The First Part of King Henry the Fourth
Prince

I know you all, and will a-while uphold
1.2.195–217

Background: having joked with Falstaffe and Poines in prose, and
seemingly planned a robbery, Hal is left alone, where, in verse for
the first time in the play, he reveals his underlying motives for indulging in the disreputable behaviour for which he is so well known
and so often condemned.

Style: solo

Where: unspecified, some texts suggest the Prince's apartments or
house

To Whom: self and audience address

# of Lines: 23

Probable Timing: 1.10 minutes

Take Note: At first glance the speech seems almost totally emotional
throughout (3/18) especially when two of the four pieces of major
punctuation are (emotional) semicolons, yet F's orthography reveals moments of great calm underneath pointing, to a speech of
enormous seriousness and resolution.

Prince

1   I know you all, and will a-while uphold
    The unyok'd humor of your idleness ,
    Yet herein will I imitate the sun ,
    Who doth permit the base contagious clouds
    To smother up his beauty from the world,
    That when he please again to be himself ,
    Being wanted, he may be more wond'red at
    By breaking through the foul and ugly mists
    Of vapors that did seem to strangle him .

2   If all the year were playing holidays ,
    To sport, would be as tedious as to work ;
    But when they seldom come, they wish'd-for come,
    And nothing pleaseth but rare accidents .

3   So when this loose behavior I throw off
    And pay the debt I never promised,
    By how much better [than] my word I am,
    By so much shall I falsify men's hopes,
    And like bright metal on a sullen ground,
    My reformation, glittering o'er my fault,
    Shall show more goodly and attract more eyes
    [Than] that which hath no [foil] to set it off .

4   I'll so offend, to make offense a skill,
    Redeeming time when men think least I will .

Prince

1   I know you all, and will a-while uphold
     The unyoak'd humor of your idlenesse :
     Yet heerein will I imitate the Sunne,
     Who doth permit the base contagious cloudes
     To smother up his Beauty from the world,
     That when he please againe to be himselfe,
     Being wanted, he may be more wondred at,
     By breaking through the foule and ugly mists
     Of vapours, that did seeme to strangle him .

2   If all the yeare were playing holidaies,
     To sport, would be as tedious as to worke ;
     But when they seldome come, they wisht-for come,
     And nothing pleaseth but rare accidents .

3   So when this loose behaviour I throw off,
     And pay the debt I never promised ;
     By how much better [then] my word I am,
     By so much shall I falsifie mens hopes,
     And like bright Mettall on a sullen ground :
     My reformation glittering o're my fault,
     Shall shew more goodly, and attract more eyes,
     [Then] that which hath no [soyle] to set it off .

4   Ile so offend, to make offence a skill,
     Redeeming time, when men thinke least I will .

- most of the non-embellished lines reveal why Hal is behaving as he is (see below), but one reveals the theme that runs throughout both parts of Henry the Fourth—how much Hal doesn't really want the Crown, viz. 'And pay the debt I never promised;' its importance double weighted by the (emotional) semi colon that finishes it

- the other non-embellished lines provide the spine not only of the speech, but of his actions throughout the play

     "I know you all, and will a-while…"

planning that when he is finally needed

     "Being wanted, he may be more wondred at,", since

     "And nothing pleaseth but rare accidents."

because then even though he will have to

     "…pay the debt I never promised;"

from his current actions people will discover

     "By how much better then my word I am,/By so much shall I falsifie mens hopes,… My reformation glittering o're my fault,/ Shall shew more goodly, and attract more eyes,"

therefore in the mean time

     "Ile so offend, to make offence a skill,"

- in terms of the released emotional energy of the piece, much of it comes in the first sentence (2/10 in F #1's nine lines, compared to 1/8 in the final fourteen), suggesting that the effects of the opening images of how he is apparently corrupting himself, though a chosen path of action, creates a strong emotional response in him still

The First Part of King Henry the Fourth
Hotspur/Hotspurre

Away, away you trifler : Love, I love thee not,
between 2.3.89–117

Background: bent on mounting rebellion, Hotspurre has been challenged by his wife Kate to account for his recent bad dreams. Though the start to his speech seems to be totally anti-Kate, the fact that he is prepared to take her with him on his perilous journey suggests that much of the argument that 'it's for the best she know nothing' might stem from the tactical concern that knowledge of the rebels' plan should not leak to the King's agents too soon, rather than from distrust of her.

Style: part of a two-handed scene

Where: Hotspurre's home

To Whom: his wife Kate

# of Lines: 23

Probable Timing: 1.10 minutes

Take Note: The speech and scene are usually played as yet another example of Hotspurre's wildness and game playing, matched in style by his equally passionate wife. Yet, for an apparently emotional moment, there are far fewer excesses than one would expect (only 14/8 in twenty-three lines). As a consequence there are many non-embellished moments that fall into three different strands, and which, when put together, suggest the possibility of a very interesting, though perhaps too fanciful, subtext.

Hotspur

1   Away,
    Away, you trifler !

2   Love, I love thee not,
    I care not for thee, Kate .

3   This is no world
    To play with mammets and to tilt with lips .

4   We must have bloody noses and crack'd crowns ,
    And pass them current too .

5   God's me, my horse !

6   What say'st thou, Kate ?

7   What wouldst thou have with me ?

---

8   Come, wilt thou see me ride ?

9   And when I am a horseback , I will swear
    I love thee infinitely .

10   But hark you, Kate,
    I must not have you henceforth question me,
    [Whither] I go, nor reason whereabout .

11 [Whither] I must, I must, and to conclude,
    This evening must I leave [you], gentle Kate .

12 I know you wise, but yet no [farther] wise
    [Than] Harry Percy's wife ; constant you are,
    But yet a woman, and for secrecy ,
    No Lady closer, for I [well] believe
    Thou wilt not utter what thou dost not know,
    And so far [will] I trust thee, gentle Kate .

---

13 Not an inch further .

14   But hark you, Kate,
    Whither I go, thither shall you go too ;
    To-day will I set forth, to-morrow you .

15 Will this content you {†} ?

Hotspurre

1 Away, away you trifler : Love, I love thee not,
I care not for thee Kate : this is no world
To play with Mammets, and to tilt with lips .

2 We must have bloodie Noses, and crack'd Crownes,
And passe them currant too .

3   Gods me, my horse .

4 What say'st thou Kate ?what wold'st thou have with me ?

5 Come, wilt thou see me ride ?

6 And when I am a horsebacke, I will sweare
I love thee infinitely .

7   But hearke you Kate,
I must not have you henceforth, question me,
[Whether] I go : nor reason whereabout .

8 [Whether] I must, I must : and to conclude,
This Evening must I leave [thee], gentle Kate .

9 I know you wise, but yet no [further] wise
[Then] Harry Percies wife .

10   Constant you are,
But yet a woman : and for secrecie,
No Lady closer .

11   For I [will] beleeve
Thou wilt not utter what thou do'st not know,
And so farre [wilt] I trust thee, gentle Kate .

12 Not an inch further .

13   But harke you Kate,
Whither I go, thither shall you go too :
To day will I set forth, to morrow you .

14 Will this content you {†} ?

- the supposed public humiliation/chastising of Kate (the opening and closing phrases of F #1); second, the repeated warning that he must not be questioned (the end of F #7) ; third, that wherever he is going, carefully avoiding saying out loud where and why, she can join him (the end of F #13 and #14), and then the short sentences

  "Gods me, my horse." plus "Come, wilt thou see me ride?" plus
    "Not an inch further." finishing with "Will this content you?"

  could suggest that it for some reason Hotspurre is determined to say nothing that can incriminate himself or Kate (is he worried Henry has a spy in the house?)

- of the limited and occasional releases the following seem of interest

  a. the opening 'put down' of Kate is intellectual, and thus seems deliberate (3/0, F #1), while the generalised testosterone of F #2 becomes passionate (2/2)

  b. then the three-sentence invitation to see him ride is very contained (1/0 , F #3-5 and the sentences unusually short (leading to the idea that they can talk without being overheard perhaps?—for the immediately following 'when' sentence, promising that he will 'sweare' he loves her 'infinitely', and the first phrase of F #7 become emotional 1/3)

  c. the warning against questioning him is non-embellished (ending of F #7), while for some reason the limited information he can give her and the need for 'secrecie' (F #8-10) is strongly intellectual (5/0)

  d. interestingly, the repetition of the need for secrecy (F #11) becomes, in comparison with the care in most of the speech, somewhat passionate (1/2)

  e. while the final invitation for her to join him (F #12-14) is basically non-embellished save for the opening warning of F #13, 'But harke you Kate,'

The First Part of King Henry the Fourth
Prince

Harry, the complaints I heare of thee, are grievous .
between 2.4.442–463

Background: at the height of a great and happy evening in the tavern, news has come that King Henry has summoned his wayward son Prince Hal to the palace the following day for a highly formal meeting. In front of all their friends, Falstaffe and Hal have decided to play-act the roles of both the King and Hal as a sort of rehearsal for the scolding to come. Here Hal plays his own father.

Style: one on one address for the amusement of everyone else present

Where: an Eastcheap tavern run by the Hostesse (sometimes known as Mistris Quickly)

To Whom: Falstaffe, in front of Falstaffe's own men Gadshill, Peto, and Bardolph; Poines; the Hostesse; the Vintner; various servers including Francis; and perhaps other tavern clientele

# of Lines: 18

Probable Timing: 0.55 minutes

Take Note: Once more modern texts revamp F's onrushed sentence structure, creating four part grammatical order out of the much longer F #2—the original setting suggesting that, for whatever reason, Hal cannot stop himself once his public destruction of Falstaffe begins.

Prince

1   {†} Harry, {†}the complaints I hear of thee are grievous .

---

2   {†} {U}ngracious boy {!} henceforth
ne'er look on me .

3   Thou art violently carried away from
grace, there is a devil haunts thee, in the likeness of an
[old fat] man, a tun of man is thy companion .

4   Why
dost thou converse with that trunk of humors, that
bolting—hutch of beastliness , that swoll'n parcel of
dropsies, that huge bombard of sack , that stuff'd cloak -
bag of guts, that roasted Manning- tree ox with the
pudding in his belly, that reverend Vice, that grey Ini-
quity , that father ruffian, that vanity in years ?

5   Wherein is he good, but to taste sack and drink it ? wherein
neat and cleanly, but to carve a capon and eat it ?where-
in cunning, but in craft ? wherein crafty , but in villainy ? wherein villainous , but in all things ?wherein worthy, but in nothing ?

---

6   That villainous abominable misleader of
youth, Falstaff , that old white-bearded Satan .

Prince

1   {†} Harry, {†}the complaints I heare of thee, are grievous .

---

2   {†} {U}ngracious Boy {?} henceforth
ne're looke on me : thou art violently carryed away from
Grace : there is a Devill haunts thee, in the likenesse of a
[fat old] Man ; a Tunne of Man is thy Companion : Why
do'st thou converse with that Trunke of Humors, that
Boulting-Hutch of Beastlinesse, that swolne Parcell of
Dropsies, that huge Bombard of Sacke, that stuft Cloake-
bagge of Guts, that rosted Manning Tree Oxe with the
Pudding in his Belly, that reverend Vice, that grey Ini-
quitie, that Father Ruffian, that Vanitie in yeeres ? wherein is he good, but to taste Sacke, and drinke it ? wherein
neat and cleanly, but to carve a Capon, and eat it ? wherein Cunning, but in Craft ?wherein Craftie, but in Villanie ? wherein Villanous, but in all things ? wherein worthy, but in nothing ?

---

3   That villanous abhominable mis-leader of
Youth, Falstaffe, that old white-bearded Sathan.

- though supposedly game playing, the surround phrases opening F #2 speak the truth as to the real world Hal and Falstaffe are currently mocking

  > " . Ungracious Boy {?} henceforth ne're looke on me : thou art violently carryed away from Grace : there is a Devill haunts thee, in the likenesse of a [fat old] Man ; a Tunne of Man is thy Companion : "

  the whole being splendidly passionate (7/5 in just three and a half lines)

- that what follows might be a foreshadowing of Hal, as the newly crowned King Henry V, rejecting Falstaffe at the end of Henry the Fourth Part 2 might be seen in

  a. after the last colon in F #2 (line four), the next passage pulling Falstaffe's physical attributes apart is full of release, especially intellectual (23/12 in just seven lines)

  b. the three lines leading to the non-embellished ending pointing out how Falstaffe's few good qualities are all serving sensual and/ or corrupt ends, is completely intellectual (6/0)

  c. the ending of F #2's itemized character assassination, summing up Falstaffe's total worth, is made up of totally unembellished phrases, as if the basic truth has been revealed at last

  > "but in all things? wherein worthy, but in nothing?"

- and the short overall summary is strongly passionate (3/3 in just the two lines of F #3)

The First Part of King Henry the Fourth
Hotspur/Hotspurre

I cannot chuse : sometime he angers me,
3.1.146–162

Background: seeking support to install Mortimer as the rightful King in place of Henry, the rebels have met at the home of the leader of the Welsh faction, Glendower, who is accounted a powerful magician—as he never fails to brag to anyone who will listen, much to Hotspurre's impatient annoyance. The following is triggered by Mortimer's mild chiding of Hotspurre, 'Fie, Cousin Percy, how you crosse my Father' ('Father' in the sense that Mortimer is married to Glendower's daughter).

Style: as part of a three-handed scene

Where: in Wales, unspecified, but presumably at the home of Glendower

To Whom: Mortimer and Worcester

# of Lines: 17

Probable Timing: 0.55 minutes

Take Note: For a short speech there is much release (28/21 in just seventeen lines): there are also ten extra breath-thoughts. Whether all of these are signs of frustration and exasperation, or more a sense of fun, or a mixture of both, is up to each actor to explore.

Hotspur

1   I cannot choose .

2   Sometime he angers me
With telling me of the moldwarp and the ant,
Of the dreamer Merlin and his prophecies,
And of a dragon, and a finless fish,
A clip -wing'd griffin and a moulten raven,
A couching lion and a ramping cat,
And such a deal of skimble-skamble stuff
As puts me from my faith .

3   I tell you what :
He held me last night at least nine hours ,
In reckoning up the several devils' names
That were his lackeys .

4   I cried "hum," and "well, go to ,"
But mark'd him not a word .

5   O, he is as tedious
As a tired horse, a railing wife ,
Worse [than] a smoky house .

6   I had rather live
With cheese and garlic in a windmill, far ,
[Than] feed on cates and have him talk to me
In any summer- house in Christendom .

Hotspurre

1   I cannot chuse : sometime he angers me,
    With telling me of the Moldwarpe and the Ant,
    Of the Dreamer Merlin, and his Prophecies ;
    And of a Dragon, and a finne-lesse Fish,
    A clip-wing'd Griffin, and a moulten Raven,
    A couching Lyon, and a ramping Cat,
    And such a deale of skimble-skamble Stuffe,
    As puts me from my Faith .

2   I tell you what,
    He held me last Night, at least, nine howres,
    In reckning up the severall Devils Names,
    That were his Lacqueyes :
    I cry'd hum, and well, goe too,
    But mark'd him not a word .

3   O, he is as tedious
    As a tyred Horse, a rayling Wife,
    Worse [then] a smoakie House .

4   I had rather live
    With Cheese and Garlick in a Windmill farre,
    [Then] feede on Cates, and have him talke to me,
    In any Summer-House in Christendome .

- much depends upon the interpretation of the surround phrase that opens the speech, '. I cannot chuse : ', for it could be angry, or, as with the teasing sequence with his wife (earlier speech) it could be that he means he cannot stop himself from pushing people to the edge—the latter may not be as fanciful as it first seems, especially if the other surround phrase ending F #2 is taken into account

    " : I cry'd hum, and well, goe too,/But mark'd him not a word . "

- describing his initial anger, F #1 opens strongly intellectually (5/1 in just three lines) and then, triggered by the only (emotional) semicolon of the speech, his listing of the generalities that annoy him turns far more passionate (8/4 in just four and a half lines)

- and the passion continues through the recounting of what happened the previous night (F #2, 4/4)

- whatever the release (humour or anger) the seven extra breath-thoughts in these two listings add fine tuning to the ludicrous de-tails, while the fact that the two opening F sentences are onrushed suggests a greater need for release than do most modern texts that grammatically split both sentences in two

- passion continues through the dismissal of Glendower as 'tedious' (3/3, F #3) and the lengths he would go to avoid being left alone with him (7/5, F #4)

The First Part of King Henry the Fourth

Prince

In both [our] Armies, there is many a soule
5.1.84–100

Background: at what turns out to be a futile meeting to avoid civil war, Hal makes a chivalric offer to prevent wide-spread bloodshed. He proposes a single combat to the death to decide the battle's winner, the combatants being himself and the man with whom he is so unfavourably compared, Hotspurre, a key rebel leader.

Style: general address for the whole group

Where: the King's camp

To Whom: the King and Worcester, in front of Hal's brother John, and loyalists Westmerland, Blunt, and Falstaffe

# of Lines: 18

Probable Timing: 1.00 minutes

Take Note: While the offer of hand to hand combat may be based on chivalry and thus encourage readers and actors alike to place the speech in the category of intellectually noble, the opening sentence suggests that this may not be so, for F #1 is emotional (1/4), and though the long-spellings relate to the men who would otherwise die in the forthcoming battle, it may not be too fanciful to suggest that Hal is not necessarily confident of success.

Prince

1   In both [your] armies there is many a soul
Shall pay full dearly for this encounter,
If once they join in trial .

2   Tell your nephew
The Prince of Wales doth join with all the world
In praise of Henry Percy .

3   By my hopes,
This present enterprise set off his head,
I do not think a braver gentleman,
More active, valiant, or more valiant, young ,
More daring or more bold, is now alive
To grace this latter age with noble deeds .

4   For my part, I may speak it to my shame,
I have a truant been to chivalry,
And so I hear , he doth account me too ;
Yet this before my father's Majesty :
I am content that he shall take the odds
Of his great name and estimation,
And will, to save the blood on either side,
Try fortune with him in a single fight .

Prince

1   In both [our] Armies, there is many a soule
     Shall pay full dearely for this encounter,
     If once they joyne in triall .

2   Tell your Nephew,
     The Prince of Wales doth joyne with all the world
     In praise of Henry Percie : By my Hopes,
     This present enterprize set off his head,
     I do not thinke a braver Gentleman,
     More active, valiant, or more valiant yong,
     More daring, or more bold, is now alive,
     To grace this latter Age with Noble deeds .

3   For my part, I may speake it to my shame,
     I have a Truant beene to Chivalry,
     And so I heare, he doth account me too :
     Yet this before my Fathers Majesty,
     I am content that he shall take the oddes
     Of his great name and estimation,
     And will, to save the blood on either side,
     Try fortune with him, in a Single Fight .

- despite the strong mental discipline of F #2's challenge and praise of Hotspurre (10/3), the fact that it is onrushed again suggests that Hal may not yet be quite as in control of himself as modern texts would like, for most of them separate the challenge as a much more in-control single sentence (mt. #2) and the praise as another (mt. #3)—implying a rational shape which the original text did not show

- interestingly, the apology for his own lack of chivalry that opens F #3 contains more emotion than intellect (2/3 in the first three lines), perhaps suggesting an honest apology rather than a mere intellectual formality

- though he does manage to recover mental self-control by the end of the speech (the last five lines of F #3), the extra breath-thought in the last line, before announcing the important capitalized 'Single Fight', could either be there to give greater rhetorical weight to the announcement, or, on a more personal level, to give a moment for steadying himself before committing to a very public and brave act (if this latter were so, it would match a similar extra-breath setting in the opening line)

The First Part of King Henry the Fourth
Hotspur/Hotspurre

Oh Harry, thou hast rob'd me of my youth :
5.4.1–86

Background: Hal's challenge to single combat was blocked by his father. Nevertheless Hal and Hotspurre (Harry Percy) have met in battle, and Hotspurre has prophetically forecast 'the houre is come/ To end the one of us' for he has been mortally wounded. This is his dying speech.

Style: part of a two-handed scene

Where: the battlefield

To Whom: Hal

# of Lines: 10

Probable Timing: 0.55 minutes

Take Note: F's two sentences suggest that ,whatever energy Hotspurre has left, the words come tumbling out in a stream, before he loses focus. Modern texts reset the speech as six sentences, creating much more difficulty for Hotspurre to put thoughts together while at the same time making him more rational than originally set.

Hotspur

1   O Harry, thou hast robb'd me of my youth !

2   I better brook the loss of brittle life
    [Than] those proud titles thou hast won of me .

3   They wound my thoughts worse [than thy] sword my
                                                       flesh .

4   But thoughts, the slave of life, and life, time's fool ,
    And time, that takes survey of all the world,
    Must have a stop .

5   O, I could prophesy ,
    But that the [earthy] and [ ] cold hand of death
    Lies on my tongue .

6   No, Percy, thou art dust
    And food for ———

Hotspurre

1   Oh Harry, thou hast rob'd me of my youth :
    I better brooke the losse of brittle life,
    [Then] those proud Titles thou hast wonne of me,
    They wound my thoghts worse, [then the] sword my
                              flesh :
    But thought's the slave of Life, and Life, Times foole ;
    And Time, that takes survey of all the world,
    Must have a stop .

2   O, I could Prophesie,
    But that the [Earth], and [the] cold hand of death,
    Lyes on my Tongue : No Percy, thou art dust
    And food for ———

- the surround phrases enhance the speech's content

   " . Oh Harry, thou hast rob'd me of my youth : "

   " : But thought's the slave of Life, and Life, Times foole ; "

   " : No Percy, thou art dust/And food for—"

- overall F #1 seems passionate, but splits in two—opening passionately (5/5 in the opening five lines), enhanced by the emotional semicolon that finishes the segment; and then becoming factual as he realises for him 'Time' 'must have a stop' (1/0, F #1's last line and a half)

- which leads to F #2 being even more factual, perhaps as if he were focusing all his energies on making his last words meaningful (5/1)

The First Part of King Henry the Fourth
Prince

For Wormes, brave Percy ./[Farewell] great heart :
5.4.87–101

Background: Hal's challenge to single combat was blocked by his father. Nevertheless Hal and Hotspurre (Harry Percy) have met in battle, and Hotspurre has been mortally wounded. As he dies, his final uncompleted sentence ends with 'Percy, thou art dust/And food for...' (see prior speech), a sentence Hal now completes.

Style: solo, to a dead body

Where: on the battlefield

To Whom: the dead Hotspurre

# of Lines: 15

Probable Timing: 0.50 minutes

Take Note: The surround phrases making up F #2 sum up Hal's response—" . Farewell great heart : /Ill-weav'd Ambition, how much art thou shrunke ? "

Prince

1   For worms , brave Percy .

2   [Fare thee well], great heart !

3   Ill-weav'd ambition, how much art thou shrunk !

4   When that this body did contain a spirit,
    A kingdom for it was too small a bound,
    But now two paces of the vilest earth
    Is room enough .

5   This earth that bears [thee] dead
    Bears not alive so stout a gentleman .

6   If thou wer't sensible of courtesy ,
    I should not make so [dear] a show of zeal ;
    But let my favors hide thy mangled face,
    And even in thy behalf I'll thank myself
    For doing these fair rites of tenderness .

7   Adieu, and take thy praise with thee to heaven,
    Thy [ignominy] sleep with thee in the grave,
    But not rememb'red in thy epitaph !

Prince

1   For Wormes, brave Percy .

2   [Farewell] great heart :
     Ill-weav'd Ambition, how much art thou shrunke ?

3   When that this bodie did containe a spirit,
     A Kingdome for it was too small a bound :
     But now two paces of the vilest Earth
     Is roome enough .

4   This Earth that beares [the] dead,
     Beares not alive so stout a Gentleman,
     If thou wer't sensible of curtesie,
     I should not make so [great] a shew of Zeale .

5   But let my favours hide thy mangled face,
     And even in thy behalfe, Ile thanke my selfe
     For doing these fayre Rites of Tendernesse .

6   Adieu, and take thy praise with thee to heaven,
     Thy [ignomy] sleepe with thee in the grave,
     But not remembred in thy Epitaph .

- surprisingly, after hand to hand combat with Hotspurre and killing the man he regards as brave and valiant even if a rebel, the speech opens with almost matching intellect and emotion (8/9 in the nine lines of the first four sentences)

- the passionate opening also causes some loss of rhetorical control, first seen in Hal's F #2 non grammatical connecting of bidding adieu to Hotspurre to the shrinking of Hotspurre's? (all men's?) 'ill-weav'd Ambition', linking it via the colon—which is somewhat disturbing and more onrushed than most modern texts would like, for they split the points into separate sentences

- modern texts also rework of F #4-5, standardising what are obviously difficult moments for him:

  a. F #4's fast-link comma (at the end of line two), where the praise of Hotspurre is suddenly coupled with what seems almost an apology for being so fulsome in the praise, is wiped out by modern texts' creating a new sentence at F #4's comma

  b. Hal's chivalric courtesy in dignifying Hotspurre's body with his own 'favours' (i.e. his personal colours, or scarf) is given a new sentence in F #5 as befits such a fine decision: most modern texts spoil the moment by folding the action into its previous mt. #6

- and in this separate action, at least in F, so emotion finally creeps in (3/7, F #5-6)

The Second Part of King Henry the Fourth
Prince {Henry}

This new, and gorgeous Garment, Majesty,
5.2.44–61

Background: Henry has died, and Hal is now King, much to the consternation of his three brothers and his father's key advisors, especially the Lord Chiefe Justice who once had occasion to imprison Hal. The following are Hal's first words as King, made in response to the Lord Chiefe Justice's greeting 'Good morrow: and heaven save your Majesty'.

Style: a group address, and to various members therein

Where: the palace at Westminster

To Whom: initially the Lord Chiefe Justice, and then almost immediately to Hal's brothers John (Lancaster), Thomas (Clarence), and Humphrey (Gloucester); and Warwicke

# of Lines: 18

Probable Timing: 1.00 minutes

Take Note: In dealing with his brothers, F shows the newly crowned Hal struggling to prevent passion swamping his intellectual sense of self.

Prince

1   This new, and gorgeous garment, majesty,
    Sits not so easy on me as you think .

2   Brothers, you mix your sadness with some fear :
    This is the English, not the Turkish court,
    Not [Amurath], an [Amurath] succeeds,
    But Harry Harry .

3   Yet be sad, good brothers,
    For ([by my faith]) it very well becomes you .
    Sorrow so royally in you appears
    That I will deeply put the fashion on
    And wear it in my heart .

4   Why then be sad,
    But entertain no more of it, good brothers,
    [Than] a joint burden laid upon us all .

5   For me, by heaven (I bid you be assur'd),
    I'll be your father and your brother too .

6   Let me but bear your love, I'll bear your cares .

7   [Yet] weep that Harry's dead, and so will I,
    But Harry lives, that shall convert those tears
    By number into hours of happiness .

Prince

1   This new, and gorgeous Garment, Majesty,
     Sits not so easie on me, as you thinke .

2   Brothers, you mixe your Sadnesse with some Feare :
     This is the English, not the Turkish Court :
     Not [Amurah], an [Amurah] succeeds,
     But Harry, Harry:Yet be sad (good Brothers)
     For ([to speake truth]) it very well becomes you :
     Sorrow, so Royally in you appeares,
     That I will deeply put the Fashion on,
     And weare it in my heart .

3   Why then be sad,
     But entertaine no more of it (good Brothers)
     [Then] a joynt burthen, laid upon us all .

4   For me, by Heaven (I bid you be assur'd)
     Ile be your Father, and your Brother too :
     Let me but beare your Love, Ile beare your Cares ;
     [But] weepe that Harrie's dead, and so will I .

5   But Harry lives, that shall convert those Teares
     By number, into houres of Happinesse .

- Hal's message to his fearful brothers, and his sorrow, is made abundantly clear by the surround phrases

  " . Brothers, you mixe your Sadnesse with some Feare : /This
    is the English, not the Turkish Court : Not Amurah, an
    Amurahsucceeds,/But Harry, Harry : Yet be sad (good
    Brothers)/For ([to speake truth]) it very well becomes you : "

  " : Let me but beare your Love, Ile beare your Cares ; /But weepe
    that Harrie's dead, and so will I . "

- Hal is passionate as he tries to explain how strange he feels, and how his brothers should not fear him is (4/4 F #1 and the first line of F #2)

- in the attempt to explain that he is still Harry and not some despotic murderer he uses all the intellect he possibly can (7/0 in just two and a half lines, line two through the first phrase of line four, F #2), yet at the same time the sentence onrushes, Hal reverts to passion as he joins in their sadness (5/6, the last four and half lines of F #2 plus F #3), suggesting that the opening self-control was fragile at best: most modern texts remove this by splitting F #2 into three separate and highly rational sentences, suggesting far more self-control than originally shown

- the speech finishes with the same pattern as seen in F #2, i.e. F #4's first two lines start intellectually (ending 'I'll be your Father, and your Brother too', 3/0), while the remainder (speaking of 'Love' and 'Teares') finishes passionately (6/6 in the last four lines)

The Life of Henry the Fift
King Henry

My learned Lord, we pray you to proceed,
1.2.9–32 & line 96

Background: prior to a key meeting with the French Ambassadors, which may well lead to war, Henry needs reassurance from his spiritual advisors as to whether war would be justified, especially on religious grounds. Two Bishops, with their own agenda, have been summoned and, before they speak, King Henry lays very clear guidelines for this consultation.

Style: one on one, in front of, and for the benefit of, a larger group

Where: a large meeting hall in the palace

To Whom: Bishop of Canterbury, in front of the Bishop of Ely, Henry's brothers Humfrey (Gloucester) and Thomas (Clarence), and advisors Bedford, Warwick, Westmerland, and Exeter

# of Lines: 25

Probable Timing: 1.15 minutes

Take Note: Henry's need for confirmation of the religious righteousness of his planned attack on France is underscored by F's surround phrases.

King Henry

1   My learned lord, we pray you to proceed,
    And justly and religiously unfold
    Why the law Salique , that they have in France,
    Or should, or should not, bar us in our claim ;
    And God forbid, my dear and faithful lord,
    That you should fashion, wrest, or bow your reading,
    Or nicely charge your understanding soul
    With opening titles miscreate, whose right
    Suits not in native colors with the truth ;
    For God doth know how many now in health
    Shall drop their blood in approbation
    Of what your reverence shall incite us to .

2   Therefore take heed how you impawn our person,
    How you awake our sleeping sword of war -
    We charge you, in the name of God, take heed ;
    For never two such kingdoms did contend
    Without much fall of blood, whose guiltless drops
    Are every one, a woe, a sore complaint,
    'Gainst him, whose wrongs gives edge unto the swords
    That makes such waste in brief mortality .

3   Under this conjuration speak , my lord ;
    For we will hear , note, and believe in heart,
    That what you speak is in your Conscience wash'd
    As pure as sin with baptism .

4   May I with right and conscience make this claim ?

King Henry

1   My learned Lord, we pray you to proceed,
     And justly and religiously unfold,
     Why the Law Salike, that they have in France,
     Or should or should not barre us in our Clayme :
     And God forbid, my deare and faithfull Lord,
     That you should fashion, wrest, or bow your reading,
     Or nicely charge your understanding Soule,
     With opening Titles miscreate, whose right
     Sutes not in native colours with the truth :
     For God doth know, how many now in health,
     Shall drop their blood, in approbation
     Of what your reverence shall incite us to .

2   Therefore take heed how you impawne our Person,
     How you awake our sleeping Sword of Warre ;
     We charge you in the Name of God take heed :
     For never two such Kingdomes did contend,
     Without much fall of blood, whose guiltlesse drops
     Are every one, a Woe, a sore Complaint,
     'Gainst him, whose wrongs gives edge unto the Swords,
     That makes such waste in briefe mortalitie .

3   Under this Conjuration, speake my Lord :
     For we will heare, note, and beleeve in heart,
     That what you speake, is in your Conscience washt,
     As pure as sinne with Baptisme .

---

4   May I with right and conscience make this claim ?

- the first surround phrase is extra weighted by being in part formed by the (emotional) semicolon, and in its potentially speedy release if it is delivered without any of the extra commas added by most modern texts

  " ; We charge you in the Name of God take heed : "
  followed by

  " . Under this Conjuration, speake my Lord : "

  (and whether these are demands of his newly awakened conscience, or merely distrust of his so-called spiritual advisors is up to each actor to explore)

- and the demand on the Bishop is made even greater with Henry's non-embellished lines, forbidding 'That you should fashion, wrest or bow your reading' because, via three consecutive non-embellished lines, 'For God doth know, how many now in health,/ Shall drop their blood, in approbation/Of what your reverence shall incite us to .'and demanding in the final line of the speech 'May I with right and conscience make this claim?'

- while Henry opens speech with some self control (4/1 in the first three lines of F #1), as he voices 'our Clayme' and the warning to speak true, his emotions begin to flow through and almost take over (5/6, the next six lines until the final colon of F #1), until the non-embellished lines speaking of those who will die ending the sentence

- the warning to 'take heed' becomes passionate (9/6 in all but one line of F #2 plus the first line of F #3), though charging the Bishop in 'the Name of God', the sentence's third line and the first surround phrase shown above, turns momentarily strongly intellectual (2/0)

- and then as Henry assures the Bishop that all his actions will depend upon the Bishop's words, so his emotions almost get the better of him (1/5 in the three lines ending F #3), only to recover composure with the non-embellished final line

The Life of Henry the Fift

King Henry

No, it is not possible you should love the Enemie
between 5.2.171–194

Background: having agreed in principle to a peace, Henry has left others to settle the fine details while he woos the French Princesse Katherine, chaperoned by her maid/confidant Alice. There is, however, one problem—his French is much weaker than her English, which makes courtship even more tricky than usual. Each speech is self-explanatory. This speech is a response to a direct question from Katherine herself, 'Is it possible dat I sould love de enemie of Fraunce?'prior to the next speech, #24, in an attempt to get Katherine to agree to his 'blunt' wooing, Henry finishes by speaking French, viz. 'How say you, La plus belle Katherine du monde mon trescher & devin deese'.

Style: as part of a three handed scene

Where: the French palace

To Whom: Katherine, in front of Alice

# of Lines: 15

Probable Timing: 0.50 minutes

Take Note: At the speech's start, an attempt to persuade Kate that he really is the 'Friend of France', F's orthography suggests that Henry has to work incredibly hard, though control is established by the speech's conclusion.

King Henry

1   No, it is not possible you should love the ene-
    my of France, Kate ; but in loving me, you should love
    the friend of France ; for I love France so well that I
    will not part with a village of it ; I will have it all mine .

2   And, Kate, when France is mine and I am yours, then
    your's is France and you are mine .

---

3   I will tell thee in French, which I am sure
    will hang upon my tongue like a new married wife
    about her husband's neck , hardly to be shook off .

4   *Je*
    quand sur le possession de France , & quand vous avez le pos-
    session de moi—let me see, what then ?

5   Saint Denis be
    my speed ! *donc vostre est France & vous êtes mienne .*

6   It is as easy for me, Kate, to conquer the kingdom as to
    speak so much more French .

7   I shall never move thee in
    French, unless it be to laugh at me .

---

8   But, Kate, dost
    thou understand thus much English ?

9   Canst thou love
    me ?

King Henry

1   No, it is not possible you should love the Enemie of France, Kate ; but in loving me, you should love
the Friend of France : for I love France so well that I
will not part with a Village of it ; I will have it all mine :
and Kate when France is mine, and I am yours ; then
yours is France, and you are mine .

2   I will tell thee in French which I am sure
will hang upon my tongue, like a new married Wife
about her Husbands Necke, hardly to be shooke off ; *Je*
quand sur le possession de Fraunce , & quand vous aves le pos-
session de moy, (Let me see, what then ?

3   Saint Dennis bee
my speede) *Donc vostre est Fraunce, & vous estes mienne .*

4   It is as easie for me, Kate, to conquer the Kingdome, as to
speake so much more French : I shall never move thee in
French, unlesse it be to laugh at me .

5   But Kate, doo'st
thou understand thus much English ?

6   Canst thou love
mee ?

- in the opening onrushed sentence there are five pieces of major punctuation, including three (emotional) semicolons, two extra breath-thoughts in the last two lines to help clarify, and absolutely no long spellings (10/0, F #1)

- the intellectual control continues as he resolves to explain what he has just said to her in French (4/1, the first two lines of F #2)

- then emotion and intellect battle as he attempts to do so (10/10 in the five and a half lines till the end of F #4)

- and then he seems to get hold of himself, for in preparing to ask her once more "Canst thou love mee?", though the speech ends with two short sentences denoting the pushing aside of anything inessential, the lead up is intellectual (2/1, F #5) and then the question non-embellished and monosyllabic (F#6)

The Life of Henry the Fift
King Henry

Now fye upon my false French : by mine Honor
5.2.220–246

Background: having agreed in principle to a peace, Henry has left others to settle the fine details while he woos the French Princesse Katherine, chaperoned by her maid/confidant Alice. There is, however, one problem—his French is much weaker than her English, which makes courtship even more tricky than usual. Following upon the previous speech, Katherine has replied 'Your Majestie ave fause Frenche enough to deceive de most sage Damoiseil dat is en Fraunce', which triggers this response.

Style: part of a three handed scene

Where: the French palace

To Whom: Katherine, in front of Alice

# of Lines: 27

Probable Timing: 1.20 minutes

Take Note: F's orthography separates the speech into two distinct parts.

King Henry

1   Now fie upon my false French!

2   By mine honor, in
true English, I love thee, Kate ; by which honor I dare
not swear thou lovest me, yet my blood begins to flatter me that thou dost—notwithstanding the poor and
untempering effect of my visage .

3   Now beshrew my
father's ambition ! he was thinking of civil wars
when he got me ; therefore was I created with a stub-
born outside, with an aspect of iron, that when I come
to woo ladies , I fright them .

4   But in faith, Kate, the elder I wax, the better I shall appear .

5   My comfort is, that
old age, that ill layer up of beauty , can do no more
spoil upon my face .

6   Thou hast me, if thou hast me, at
the worst ; and thou shalt wear me, if thou wear me,
better and better ; and therefore tell me, most faire Katherine, will you have me ?

7   Put off your maiden blushes,
avouch the thoughts of your heart with the looks of
an empress , take me by the hand, and say, "Harry of
England, I am thine" ; which word thou shalt no sooner
bless mine ear withal , but I will tell thee aloud , "England is thine, Ireland is thine, France is thine, and Henry
[Plantagenet] is thine" ; who, though I speak it before his
face, if he be not fellow with the best king, thou shalt
find the best king of good fellows .

8   Come, your an-
swer in broken music ; for thy voice is music and
thy English broken ; therefore, queen of all, Katherine,
break thy mind to me in broken English—wilt thou
have me ?

King Henry

1   Now fye upon my false French : by mine Honor in
true English, I love thee Kate ; by which Honor, I dare
not sweare thou lovest me, yet my blood begins to flatter me, that thou doo'st ; notwithstanding the poore and
untempering effect of my Visage .

2   Now beshrew my
Fathers Ambition, hee was thinking of Civill Warres
when hee got me, therefore was I created with a stub-
borne out-side, with an aspect of Iron, that when I come
to wooe Ladyes, I fright them : but in faith Kate, the elder I wax, the better I shall appeare .

3   My comfort is, that
Old Age, that ill layer up of Beautie, can doe no more
spoyle upon my Face .

4   Thou hast me, if thou hast me, at
the worst ;and thou shalt weare me, if thou weare me,
better and better : and therefore tell me, most faire Katherine, will you have me ?

5   Put off your Maiden Blushes,
avouch the Thoughts of your Heart with the Lookes of
an Empresse, take me by the Hand, and say, Harry of
England, I am thine : which Word thou shalt no sooner
blesse mine Eare withall, but I will tell thee alowd, England is thine, Ireland is thine, France is thine, and Henry
[Plantaginet] is thine ; who, though I speake it before his
Face, if he be not Fellow with the best King, thou shalt
finde the best King of Good-fellowes .

6   Come your Answer in broken Musick ; for thy Voyce is Musick, and
thy English broken : Therefore Queene of all, Katherine,
breake thy minde to me in broken English ; wilt thou
have me ?

- the depth of Henry's request can be seen in the repetition of virtually the same question in widely separated, quadruply weighted, non-embellished, monosyllabic surround phrases both incorporated in part with an emotional semicolon

　" . Thou hast me, if thou hast me, at the worst ; "
and
　" ; wilt thou have me ? "

- the surround phrases reiterate the two main strands of Henry's wooing, first that he does love Kate
and the fact he's not particularly good-looking
the two strands eventually joining

　" . Thou hast me, if thou hast me, at the worst ; and thou shalt
　　weare me, if thou weare me, better and better : and therefore
　　tell me, most faire Katherine, will you have me ? "
leading yet again to the final request

　" . Come your Answer in broken Musick ; for thy Voyce is
　　Musick, and thy English broken : Therefore Queene of all,
　　Katherine, breake thy minde to me in broken English ; wilt
　　thou have me ? "

- the first half of the speech, essentially summarising all that has been said before vis à vis his love and his unprepossessing appearance is onrushed and passionate (17/17, F #1-4), suggesting that Henry is not yet in complete control of himself: most modern texts split each of F#1-2 in two, thus suggesting more control than might yet be established, which robs the second half of F's setting of the speech, which offers the possibilityn that Henry eventually does succeed in regaining some self-control, but not until half way though the speech, and not consistently

- as he asks her to 'Put off your Maiden Blushes', so his intellect takes over (9/2, the first three lines of F #5), while the imagination running rampant at the thought of her saying yes triggers his emotions a little more (12/7 until the end of the sentence)

- and passion returns as he asks for her answer in 'broken Musick' (9/6, all but the last line of F #6), until the final non-embellished phrase

The Life of King Henry the Eight
Surrey

Thou art a proud Traitor, Priest .Thy Ambition
between 3.2.252–344

Background: thanks to the King's withdrawal of support for Wolsey, Surrey, a second son-in-law of the recently unjustly executed Duke of Buckingham, can finally speak his mind directly to Wolsey's face, and does. One note; for optimum results it might be best to split the speech in two, and audition with either sentences #1-4 or #4-7.

Style: one on one in front of a very interested small group of supporters

Where: unspecified, but presumably the palace

To Whom: to Wolsey, in front of the equally anti-Wolsey nobles, Norfolke, Suffolke and the Lord Chamberlaine

# of Lines: 27

Probable Timing: 1.20 minutes

Take Note: The opening and closing short sentences say all that everyone opposed to Wolsey or who have suffered at his hands wants him to hear: as such the speech is remarkably self-controlled (40/10 overall). Thus the few signs of cracks in the sustained intellectual attack are well worth focusing on.

Surrey

1　Thou art a proud traitor, priest .

2　　　　　　　　　　　　　Thy ambition,
　Thou scarlet sin , robb'd this bewailing land
　Of noble Buckingham, my father-in- law;
　The heads of all thy brother- cardinals
　(With thee and all thy best parts bound together)
　Weigh'd not a hair of his .

3　　　　　　　　　　　　Plague of your policy !

4　You sent me deputy for Ireland,
　Far from his succor , from the King, from all
　That might have mercy on the fault thou gav'st him ;
　Whil'st your great goodness , out of holy pity ,
　Absolv'd him with an axe .

5　　　　　　　　　　By my soul ,
　Your long coat, priest, protects you, thou should'st feel
　My sword i'th'life blood of thee else .

6　My Lord of Norfolk , as you are truly noble,
　As you respect the common good, the state
　Of our despis'd nobility , our issues
　([Who], if he live, will scarce be gentlemen),
　Produce the grand sum of his sins , the articles
　Collected from his life .

7　{†} Lord Cardinal , the King's {†} pleasure is—
　Because all those things you have done of late
　By your power legative within this kingdom
　Fall into'th'compass of a præmunire -
　That therefore such a writ be sued against you,
　To forfeit all your goods, lands, tenements,
　[Chattels], and whatsoever, and to be
　Out of the King's protection .

8　　　　　　　　　　　This is my charge .

Surrey

1   Thou art a proud Traitor, Priest .

2   Thy Ambition
     (Thou Scarlet sinne) robb'd this bewailing Land
     Of Noble Buckingham, my Father-in-Law,
     The heads of all thy Brother-Cardinals,
     (With thee, and all thy best parts bound together)
     Weigh'd not a haire of his .

3   Plague of your policie,
     You sent me Deputie for Ireland,
     Farre from his succour ; from the King, from all
     That might have mercie on the fault, thou gav'st him :
     Whil'st your great Goodnesse, out of holy pitty,
     Absolv'd him with an Axe .

4   By my Soule,
     Your long Coat (Priest) protects you,
     Thou should'st feele
     My Sword i'th'life blood of thee else .

5   My Lord of Norfolke, as you are truly Noble,
     As you respect the common good, the State
     Of our despis'd Nobilitie, our Issues,
     ([Whom] if he live, will scarse be Gentlemen)
     Produce the grand summe of his sinnes, the Articles
     Collected from his life .

6   {†} Lord Cardinall, the Kings {†} pleasure is,
     Because all those things you have done of late
     By your power Legative within this Kingdome,
     Fall into'th'compasse of a Premunire ;
     That therefore such a Writ be sued against you,
     To forfeit all your Goods, Lands, Tenements,
     [Castles], and whatsoever, and to be
     Out of the Kings protection .

7   This is my Charge.

- as Surrey describes Wolsey as being of far less worth than the men he had beheaded (Surrey's father-in-law Buckingham and Wolsey's 'Brother-Cardinalls'), the two extra breath-thoughts in F #2 suggest that he has difficulty in controlling himself

- the onrushed sentence and emotional semicolon add weight to the fact that F #3 is passionate (5/4), all highlighting Surrey's personal grounds for loathing Wolsey (for separating him from the King by sending him to Ireland, thus rendering him unable to help his father-in-law when Wolsey attacked him)

- that Surrey's statement that he can barely prevent himself from drawing his sword and stabbing Wolsey should not be dismissed as mere rhetoric but taken seriously can be seen in the split line set in F #4, which essentially forces him to pause before continuing

- the final semicolon emphasises Surrey's emotions in handing to Wolsey the formal instrument by which he will be destroyed, the writ of 'præmunire/Premunire'—a device summoning Wolsey before a royal court on a charge of asserting that a sovereign's absolute authority is inferior to that of the Pope (if Wolsey is found guilty, it could strip him of all his possessions and perhaps his freedoms too)

BIBLIOGRAPHY

The most easily accessible general information is to be found under the citations of *Campbell,* and of *Halliday.* The finest summation of matters academic is to be found within the all-encompassing *A Textual Companion,* listed below in the first part of the bibliography under *Wells, Stanley and Taylor, Gary* (eds.)

Individual modem editions consulted are listed below under the separate headings 'The Complete Works in Compendium Format' and 'The Complete Works in Separate Individual Volumes,' from which the modem text audition speeches have been collated and compiled.

All modem act, scene, and/or line numbers refer the reader to *The Riverside Shakespeare,* in my opinion still the best of the complete works, despite the excellent compendiums that have been published since.

The F/Q material is taken from a variety of already published sources, including not only all the texts listed in the 'Photostatted Reproductions in Compendium Format' below, but also earlier individually printed volumes, such as the twentieth century editions published under the collective title *The Facsimiles of Plays from The First Folio of Shakespeare* by Faber & Gwyer, and the nineteenth century editions published on behalf of The New Shakespere Society.

The heading 'Single Volumes of Special Interest' is offered to newcomers to Shakespeare in the hope that the books may add useful knowledge about the background and craft of this most fascinating of theatrical figures.

PHOTOSTATTED REPRODUCTIONS OF THE ORIGINAL TEXTS IN COMPENDIUM FORMAT

Allen, M.J.B. and K. Muir, (eds.). *Shakespeare's Plays in Quarto.* Berkeley: University of California Press, 1981.

Blaney, Peter (ed.). *The Norton Facsimile (The First Folio of Shakespeare).* New York: W.W.Norton & Co., Inc., 1996 (see also Hinman, below).

Brewer D.S. (ed.). *Mr. William Shakespeare's Comedies, Histories & Tragedies, The Second/Third/Fourth Folio Reproduced in Facsimile.* (3 vols.), 1983.

Hinman, Charlton (ed.). *The Norton Facsimile (The First Folio of Shakespeare)*. New York: W.W.Norton & Company, Inc., 1968.

Kokeritz, Helge (ed.). *Mr. William Shakespeare's Comedies, Histories & Tragedies*. New Haven: Yale University Press, 1954.

Moston, Doug (ed.). *Mr. William Shakespeare's Comedies, Histories, and Tragedies*. New York: Routledge, 1998.

MODERN TYPE VERSION OF THE FIRST FOLIO IN COMPENDIUM FORMAT

Freeman, Neil. (ed.). *The Applause First Folio of Shakespeare in Modern Type*. New York & London: Applause Books, 2001.

MODERN TEXT VERSIONS OF THE COMPLETE WORKS IN COMPENDIUM FORMAT

Craig, H. and D. Bevington (eds.). *The Complete Works of Shakespeare*. Glenview: Scott, Foresman and Company, 1973.

Evans, G.B. (ed.). *The Riverside Shakespeare*. Boston: Houghton Mifflin Company, 1974.

Wells, Stanley and Gary Taylor (eds.). *The Oxford Shakespeare, William Shakespeare , the Complete Works, Original Spelling Edition,* Oxford: The Clarendon Press, 1986.

Wells, Stanley and Gary Taylor (eds.). *The Oxford Shakespeare, William Shakespeare, The Complete Works, Modern Spelling Edition*. Oxford: The Clarendon Press, 1986.

MODERN TEXT VERSIONS OF THE COMPLETE WORKS IN SEPARATE INDIVIDUAL VOLUMES

The Arden Shakespeare. London: Methuen & Co. Ltd., Various dates, editions, and editors .

Folio Texts. Freeman, Neil H. M. (ed.) Applause First Folio Editions, 1997, and following.

The New Cambridge Shakespeare. Cambridge: Cambridge University Press. Various dates, editions, and editors.

New Variorum Editions of Shakespeare. Furness, Horace Howard (original editor.). New York: 1880, Various reprints. All these volumes have been in a state of re-editing and reprinting since they first appeared in 1880. Various dates, editions, and editors.

The Oxford Shakespeare. Wells, Stanley (general editor). Oxford: Oxford University Press, Various dates and editors.

The New Penguin Shakespeare . Harmondsworth, Middlesex: Penguin Books, Various dates and editors.

The Shakespeare Globe Acting Edition. Tucker, Patrick and Holden, Michael. (eds.). London: M.H.Publications, Various dates.

SINGLE VOLUMES OF SPECIAL INTEREST

Baldwin, T.W. *William Shakespeare's Petty School.* 1943.

Baldwin, T.W. *William Shakespeare's Small wtin and Lesse Greeke.* (2 vols.) 1944.

Barton, John. *Playing Shakespeare.* 1984.

Beckerman, Bernard. *Shakespeare at the Globe, I 599-1609.* 1962. Berryman, John. *Berryman 's Shakespeare.* 1999.

Bloom, Harold. *Shakespeare: The Invention of the Human.* 1998. Booth, Stephen (ed.). *Shakespeare's Sonnets.* 1977.

Briggs, Katharine. *An Encyclopedia of Fairies.* 1976.

Campbell, Oscar James, and Edward G. Quinn (eds.). *The Reader's Encyclopedia of Shakespeare. 1966.*

Crystal, David, and Ben Crystal. *Shakespeare's Words: A Glossary & Language Companion.* 2002.

Flatter, Richard. *Shakespeare's Producing Hand.* 1948 (reprint).

Ford, Boris. (ed.). *The Age of Shakespeare.* 1955.

Freeman, Neil H.M. *Shakespeare's First Texts.* 1994.

Greg, W.W. *The Editorial Problem in Shakespeare: A Survey of the Foundations of the Text.* 1954 (3rd. edition).

Gurr, Andrew . *Playgoing in Shakespeare's London.* 1987. Gurr, Andrew. *The Shakespearean Stage, 1574-1642.* 1987. Halliday, F.E. *A Shakespeare Companion.* 1952.

Harbage, Alfred. *Shakespeare's Audience.* 1941.

Harrison, G.B. (ed.). *The Elizabethan Journals.* 1965 (revised, 2 vols.).

Harrison, G.B. (ed.). *A Jacobean Journal.* 1941.

Harrison, G.B. (ed.). *A Second Jacobean Journal.* 1958.

Hinman, Charlton. *The Printing and Proof Reading of the First Folio of Shakespeare.* 1963 (2 vols.).

Joseph, Bertram. *Acting Shakespeare.* 1960.

Joseph, Miriam (Sister). *Shakespeare's Use of The Arts of wnguage.* 1947.

King, T.J. *Casting Shakespeare's Plays.* 1992.

Lee, Sidney and C.T. Onions. *Shakespeare's England : An Account Of The Life And Manners Of His Age.* (2 vols.) 1916.

Linklater, Kristin. *Freeing Shakespeare's Voice.* 1992.

Mahood, **M .M.** *Shakespeare's Wordplay.* 1957.

O'Connor, Gary. *William Shakespeare: A Popular Life.* 2000.

Ordish, T.F. *Early London Theatres.* 1894. (1971 reprint).

Rodenberg, Patsy. *Speaking Shakespeare.* 2002.

Schoenbaum. S. *William Shakespeare: A Documentary Life.* 1975.

Shapiro, Michael. *Children of the Revels.* 1977.

Simpson, Percy. *Shakespeare's Punctuation.* 1969 (reprint).

Smith, Irwin. *Shakespeare's Blackfriars Playhouse.* 1964.

Southern, Richard. *The Staging of Plays Before Shakespeare.* 1973.

Spevack, M. *A Complete and Systematic Concordance to the Works Of Shakespeare.* 1968-1980 (9vols.).

Tillyard, E.M.W. *The Elizabethan World Picture.* 1942.

Trevelyan, G.M. (ed.). *Illustrated English Social History.* 1942.

Vendler, Helen. *The Art of Shakespeare's Sonnets.* 1999.

Walker, Alice F. *Textual Problems of the First Folio.* 1953.

Walton, J.K. *The Quarto Copy of the First Folio.* 1971.

Warren, Michael. *William Shakespeare, The Parallel King Lear 1608-1623.*

Wells, Stanley and Taylor, Gary (eds.). *Modernising Shakespeare's Spelling, with Three Studies in The Text of Henry V.* 1975.

Wells, Stanley. *Re-Editing Shakespeare for the Modern Reader.* 1984.

Wells, Stanley and Gary Taylor (eds.). *William Shakespeare: A Textual Companion.* 1987.

Wright, George T. *Shakespeare's Metrical Art.* 1988.

HISTORICAL DOCUMENTS

Daniel, Samuel. *The Fowre Bookes of the Civile Warres Between The Howses Of Lancaster and Yorke.* 1595.

Holinshed, Raphael. *Chronicles of England, Scotland and Ireland.* 1587 (2nd. edition).

Halle, Edward. *The Union of the Two Noble and Illustre Famelies of Lancastre And Yorke.* 1548 (2nd. edition).

Henslowe, Philip: Foakes, R.A. and Rickert (eds.). *Henslowe's Diary.* 1961.

Plutarch: North, Sir Thomas (translation of a work in French prepared by Jacques Amyots). *The Lives of The Noble Grecians and Romanes.* 1579.

APPENDIX 1:
GUIDE TO THE EARLY TEXTS

A QUARTO (Q)

A single text, so called because of the book size resulting from a particular method of printing. Eighteen of Shakespeare's plays were published in this format by different publishers at various dates between 1594-1622, prior to the appearance of the 1623 Folio.

THE FIRST FOLIO (F1)'

Thirty-six of Shakespeare's plays (excluding *Pericles* and *Two Noble Kinsmen,* in which he had a hand) appeared in one volume, published in 1623. All books of this size were termed Folios, again because of the sheet size and printing method, hence this volume is referred to as the First Folio. For publishing details see Bibliography, 'Photostated Reproductions of the Original Texts.'

THE SECOND FOLIO (F2)

Scholars suggest that the Second Folio, dated 1632 but perhaps not published until 1640, has little authority, especially since it created hundreds of new problematic readings of its own. Nevertheless more than 800 modern text readings can be attributed to it. The **Third Folio** (1664) and the **Fourth Folio** (1685) have even less authority, and are rarely consulted except in cases of extreme difficulty.

APPENDIX 2:
WORD, WORDS, WORDS

PART ONE: VERBAL CONVENTIONS (AND HOW THEY WILL BE SET IN THE FOLIO TEXT)

"THEN" AND "THAN"

These two words, though their neutral vowels sound different to modern ears, were almost identical to Elizabethan speakers and readers, despite their different meanings. F and Q make little distinction between them, setting them interchangeably . The original setting will be used, and the modern reader should soon get used to substituting one for the other as necessary.

"I," "AY," AND "AYE"

F/Q often print the personal pronoun "I" and the word of agreement "aye" simply as "I." Again, the modern reader should quickly get used to this and make the substitution when necess ary. The reader should also be aware that very occasionally either word could be used and the phrase make perfect sense, even though different meanings would be implied.

"MY SELFE/HIM SELFE/HER SELFE" VERSUS "MYSELF/HIMSELF/HER-SELF"

Generally F/Q separate the two parts of the word, "my selfe" while most modern texts set the single word "myself." The difference is vital, based on Elizabethan philosophy. Elizabethans regarded themselves as composed of two parts, the corporeal "I," and the more spiritual part, the "self." Thus, when an Elizabethan character refers to "my selfe," he or she is often referring to what is to all intents and purposes a separate being, even if that being is a particular part of him- or herself. Thus soliloquies can be thought of as a debate between the "I" and "my selfe," and, in such speeches, even though there may be only one character on-stage, it's as if there were two distinct entities present.

UNUSUAL SPELLING OF REAL NAMES, BOTH OF PEOPLE AND PLACES

Real names, both of people and places, and foreign languages are often reworked for modern understanding. For example, the French town often set in Fl as "Callice" is usually reset as "Calais." F will be set as is.

NON-GRAMMATICAL USES OF VERBS IN BOTH TENSE AND APPLICATION

Modern texts 'correct' the occasional Elizabethan practice of setting a singular noun with plural verb (and vice versa), as well as the infrequent use of the past tense of a verb to describe a current situation. The F reading will be set as is, without annotation.

ALTERNATIVE SETTINGS OF A WORD WHERE DIFFERENT SPELLINGS MAINTAIN THE SAME MEANING

F/Q occasionally set what appears to modern eyes as an archaic spelling of a word for which there is a more common modern alternative, for example "murther" for murder , "burthen" for burden, "moe" for more, "vilde" for vile. Though some modern texts set the Fl (or alternative Q) setting, others modernise. Fl will be set as is with no annotation.

ALTERNATIVE SETTINGS OF A WORD WHERE DIFFERENT SPELLINGS SUGGEST DIFFERENT MEANINGS

Far more complicated is the situation where, while an Elizabethan could substitute one word formation for another and still imply the same thing, to modern eyes the substituted word has an entirely different meaning to the one it has replaced. The following is by no means an exclusive list of the more common dual-spelling, dual-meaning words

anticke-antique	mad-made	sprite-spirit
born-borne	metal-mettle	sun-sonne
hart-heart	mote-moth	travel-travaill
human-humane	pour-(po wre)-power	through-thorough
lest-least	reverent-reverend	troth-truth
lose-loose	right-rite	whether-whither

Some of these doubles offer a metrical problem too, for example "sprite," a one syllable word, versus "spirit." A potential problem occurs in *A Midsummer Nights Dream,* where the modern text s set Q1's "thorough," and thus the scansion pattern of elegant magic can be established, whereas F1's more plebeian "through" sets up a much more awkward and clumsy moment.

The F reading will be set in the Folio Text, as will the modern texts' substitution of a different word formation in the Modern Text. If the modern text substitution has the potential to alter the meaning (and sometimes scansion) of the line, it will be noted accordingly.

PART TWO: WORD FORMATIONS COUNTED AS EQUIVALENTS FOR THE FOLLOWING SPEECHES

Often the spelling differences between the original and modern texts are quite obvious, as with "she"/"shee". And sometimes Folio text passages are so flooded with longer (and sometimes shorter) spellings that, as described in the General Introduction, it would seem that vocally something unusual is taking place as the character speaks.

However, there are some words where the spelling differences are so marginal that they need not be explored any further. The following is by no mean s an exclusive list of word s that in the main will not be taken into account when discussing emotional moments in the various commentaries accompanying the audition speeches.

(modern text spelling shown first)

and- &	murder - murther	tabor - taber
apparent - apparant	mutinous - mutenous	ta'en - tane
briars - briers	naught - nought	then - than
choice - choise	obey - obay	theater - theatre
defense - defence	o'er - o're	uncurrant - uncurrent
debtor - debter	offense - offence	than - then
enchant - inchant	quaint - queint	venomous - venemous
endurance - indurance	reside - recide	virtue - vertue
ere - e'er	Saint - S.	weight - waight
expense - expence	sense - sence	
has - ha's	sepulchre - sepulcher	
heinous - hainous	show - shew	
I'11 - Ile	solicitor - soliciter	
increase - encrease	sugar - suger	

APPENDIX 3:
THE PATTERN OF MAGIC, RITUAL &
INCANTATION

THE PATTERNS OF "NORMAL" CONVERSATION

The normal pattern of a regular Shakespearean verse line is akin to five pairs of human heart beats, with ten syllables being arranged in five pairs of beats, each pair alternating a pattern of a weak stress followed by a strong stress. Thus, a normal ten syllable heartbeat line (with the emphasis on the capitalised words) would read as

weak- STRONG, weak - STRONG, weak- STRONG, weak- STRONG, weak- STRONG
(shall I com- PARE thee TO a SUMM- ers DAY)

Breaks would either be in length (under or over ten syllables) or in rhythm (any combinations of stresses other than the five pairs of weak-strong as shown above), or both together.

THE PATTERNS OF MAGIC, RITUAL, AND INCANTATION

Whenever magic is used in the Shakespeare plays the form of the spoken verse changes markedly in two ways . The length is usually reduced from ten to just seven syllables, and the pattern of stresses is completely reversed, as if the heartbeat was being forced either by the circumstances of the scene or by the need of the speaker to completely change direction. Thus in comparison to the normal line shown above, or even the occasional minor break, the more tortured and even dangerous magic or ritual line would read as

STRONG - weak, STRONG- weak, STRONG - weak, STRONG
(WHEN shall WE three MEET a GAINE)

The strain would be even more severely felt in an extended passage, as when the three weyward Sisters begin the potion that will fetch Macbeth to them. Again, the spoken emphasis is on the capitalised words and the effort of, and/or fixed determination in, speaking can clearly be felt.

> THRICE the BRINDed CAT hath MEW"D
> THRICE and ONCE the HEDGE-Pigge WHIN"D
> HARPier CRIES, 'tis TIME, 'tis TIME.

UNUSUAL ASPECTS OF MAGIC

It's not always easy for the characters to maintain it. And the magic doesn't always come when the character expects it. What is even more interesting is that while the pattern is found a lot in the Comedies, it is usually in much gentler situations, often in songs *(Two Gentlemen of Verona, Merry Wives of Windsor, Much Ado About Nothing, Twelfth Night, The Winters Tale)* and/or simplistic poetry *(Loves Labours Lost* and *As You Like It),* as well as the casket sequence in *The Merchant of Venice.*

It's too easy to dismiss these settings as inferior poetry known as doggerel. But this may be doing the moment and the character a great disservice. The language may be simplistic, but the passion and the magical/ritual intent behind it is wonderfully sincere. It's not just a matter of magic for the sake of magic, as with Pucke and Oberon enchanting mortals and Titania. It's a matter of the human heart's desires too. Orlando, in *As You Like It,* when writing peons of praise to Rosalind suggesting that she is composed of the best parts of the mythical heroines because

> THEREfore HEAVen NATure CHARG"D
> THAT one BODie SHOULD be FILL"D
> WITH all GRACes WIDE enLARG"D

And what could be better than Autolycus *(The Winters Tale)* using magic in his opening song as an extra enticement to trap the unwary into buying all his peddler's goods, ballads, and trinkets.

To help the reader, most magic/ritual lines will be bolded in the Folio text version of the speeches.

ACKNOWLEDGMENTS

Neil dedicated *The Applause First Folio in Modern Type*
"To All Who Have Gone Before"
and there are so many who have gone before in the sharing of Shakespeare through publication. Back to John Heminge and Henry Condell who published *Mr. William Shakespeares Comedies, Histories, & Tragedies* which we now know as The First Folio and so preserved 18 plays of Shakespeare which might otherwise have been lost. As they wrote in their note "To the great Variety of Readers.":

> Reade him, therefore; and againe, and againe : And if then you doe not like him, surely you are in some manifest danger, not to understand him. And so we leave you to other of his Friends, whom if you need, can be your guides: if you neede them not, you can lead yourselves, and others, and such readers we wish him.

I want to thank John Cerullo for believing in these books and helping to spread Neil's vision. I want to thank Rachel Reiss for her invaluable advice and assistance. I want to thank my wife, Maren and my family for giving me support, but above all I want to thank Julie Stockton, Neil's widow, who was able to retrive Neil's files from his old non-internet connected Mac, without which these books would not be possible. Thank you Julie.

Shakespeare for Everyone!

Paul Sugarman, April 2021

AUTHOR BIOS

Neil Freeman (1941-2015) trained as an actor at the Bristol Old Vic Theatre School. In the world of professional Shakespeare he acted in fourteen of the plays, directed twenty-four, and coached them all many times over.

His groundbreaking work in using the first printings of the Shakespeare texts in performance, on the rehearsal floor and in the classroom led to lectures at the Shakespeare Association of America and workshops at both the ATHE and VASTA, and grants/fellowships from the National Endowment for the Arts (USA), The Social Science and Humanities Research Council (Canada), and York University in Toronto. He prepared and annotated the thirty-six individual Applause First Folio editions of Shakespeare's plays and the complete *The Applause First Folio of Shakespeare in Modern Type*. For Applause he also compiled *Once More Unto the Speech, Dear Friends*, three volumes (Comedy, History and Tragedy) of Shakespeare speeches with commentary and insights to inform audition preparation.

He was Professor Emeritus in the Department of Theatre, Film and Creative Writing at the University of British Columbia, and dramaturg with The Savage God project, both in Vancouver, Canada. He also taught regularly at the National Theatre School of Canada, Concordia University, Brigham Young University.. He had a Founder's Ring (and the position of Master Teacher) with Shakespeare & Company in Lenox, Mass: he was associated with the Will Geer Theatre in Los Angeles; Bard on the Beach in Vancouver; Repercussion Theatre in Montreal; and worked with the Stratford Festival, Canada, and Shakespeare Santa Cruz.

Paul Sugarman is an actor, editor, writer, and teacher of Shakespeare. He is founder of the Instant Shakespeare Company, which has presented annual readings of all of Shakespeare's plays in New York City for over twenty years. For Applause Theatre & Cinema Books, he edited John Russell Brown's publication of *Shakescenes: Shakespeare for Two* and The Applause Shakespeare Library, as well as Neil Freeman's Applause First Folio Editions and *The Applause First Folio of Shakespeare in Modern Type*. He has published pocket editions of all of Shakespeare's plays using the original settings of the First Folio in modern type for Puck Press. Sugarman studied with Kristin Linklater and Tina Packer at Shakespeare & Company where he met Neil Freeman.